ALISON HOLST'S NEW

MICROWAVE COOKBOOK

We would like to acknowledge the help received by the following:-

Anchor Dairy Products and Crown Cream
Buttermark, N.Z. Dairy Board
Caxton Printing Works Ltd.
Coal Range Kitchen Shop
Desirée Potatoes
Diamond Pasta and Flour
Empire Spices
Ferndale Dairies of Eltham
Fleming & Co Ltd.
Fresh Fruit and Vegetable Publicity Council
Golden Coast Poultry Industries Ltd
Hansells (NZ) Ltd
Harkness & Young Ltd
Harvey Farms Chicken
Andrew Hawley Ltd
Horrobin and Hodge Herbs
Johnson's Wax N.Z. Ltd.
Lamnei Plastics, Alison Holst Microwave Dish
McCulloch Products Ltd.
Nestles (N.Z.) Ltd.
N.Z. Fishing Industry Board
N.Z. Meat Producers Board
N.Z. Potato Board
N.Z. Beef and Lamb Marketing Bureau Inc.
N.Z. Sugar Co. Ltd.
Pasta Fresca
Pork Industry Council
The Potters Shop, Tinakori Rd.
Poultry Industries Association of N.Z.
K.J. Rew & Co. Ltd.
Seasmoke Fine Fish Products
Spillane's Trading Co. Ltd., Corning Ware
Toshiba — Fairbairn Wright Ltd.
Trigon Plastics Ltd.
Turners and Growers

Contents

Fifth printing, 1989
BECKETT PUBLISHING
28 Poland Rd, Glenfield,
Auckland, New Zealand.

ISBN 0-908676-29-8

© Text Alison Holst
© Photography, Beckett Books Ltd

Design: Alison Holst & Sal Criscillo
Photography: Sal Criscillo
Typesetting: WordPlay Design & Type Ltd
Artwork: Warwick Fleury
Printed in Hong Kong through
Bookprint Consultants Ltd, Wellington.

Introduction

My microwave oven is one of the most important pieces of equipment in my kitchen. I don't know what I'd do without it!

SPEED

Using it, often in conjunction with my regular cooktop and oven, but sometimes alone, I can produce meals unbelievably quickly — often in less than half the time required by conventional methods.

For example, my favourite small roast cooks in five minutes, vegetables in seven or eight minutes, and an easy pudding or cake in five to eight minutes.

CUT FUEL COSTS

Because no preheating is required, because cooking times are short and the wattage is much less than that of a conventional stove, power savings are considerable.

COOK CREATIVELY. . .

As long as you know how to use your microwave oven properly, you can cook as creatively with it as you can with any other stove.

OR CUT CORNERS

We all have moments when inspiration fails us and we have barely enough energy to open the kitchen door, let alone cook. At such times your microwave will prove invaluable for thawing, warming or reheating, or helping you to get food into those hungry mouths with the minimum of time and effort.

REDUCE DISHWASHING

Dishwashing is dramatically reduced when you microwave meals. You find burnt pots and baked-on crusts are things of the past. What's more, you can often cook in paper packages, plastic bags, disposable containers or in the plate you will take to the table.

THE MORE THE MERRIER

Many previously 'one-cook' families turn into 'many cook' groups when a microwave oven arrives in the kitchen. Adults who have shown no previous interest in cooking, are intrigued by the technology and can follow the easy one-two-three directions. Teenagers can feed themselves independently and easily, and younger children don't have to wait too long to see the results of their efforts and are less likely to get burnt.

COOK NOW, HEAT LATER

As a food warmer, the microwave oven stars! You can cook extra the day before, prepare the main meal at the time of day that suits you best, or put aside an extra plate for the latecomer. Microwave-reheated food looks and tastes as if it has been freshly cooked.

THAW FAST

Your freezer is twice as valuable when you can thaw food in minutes rather than in hours. You don't have to plan hours ahead, nor panic when there's suddenly an extra mouth to feed.

As you look through this book you will find the recipes which I cook regularly in my microwave oven. Many of these are modifications of my "conventional" recipes.

I hope that my recipes will give you confidence to start using your microwave oven efficiently, and show you how this magic machine will simplify and speed up your meal preparation.

Alexander Holst

IMPORTANT NOTE

Cakes and baking can overcook in a short time in a microwave oven. Please make sure you read the references to baking on the following pages, before you start.

Baking times vary, as explained in these pages. Especially if you are baking in a covered pan, lifted slightly from the floor of your oven, you may find the cooking time is shorter than that suggested.

The first time you make a recipe, start checking after two thirds of the suggested time.

Make sure you have modified the cooking time if your oven has a wattage higher than 650W, and if different names are given to power levels of 30%, 50% and 70% power (see below).

Cooking Levels and Details

The wattage of domestic microwave ovens varies from 500 watts to 700 watts.

In most microwave ovens you can choose one of several different power levels when you cook.

Most of the time, you cook at full power, that is High or 100% power. If you do not specify other power levels or instructions when you cook, your microwave oven will cook at this level.

The power levels on various microwave ovens are given different names.

I have used the following names for the different power levels used in the recipes in this book.

High	100%	power ..	650 Watts
Medium-high	70%	power ..	450 Watts
Medium ...	50%	power ..	350 Watts
Defrost	30%	power ..	220 Watts

The percentages and wattages given are approximate only. My recipes were cooked and tested using a Toshiba E.R.7900 A/N 650 Watt microwave oven.

Your oven may have different settings. Don't worry! This may be overcome easily, either by using slightly shorter or longer cooking times, or by using your instruction book to find the corresponding settings for your microwave oven. The recipes in this book have been tested in an oven with a turntable. If you prepare these recipes in an older oven without a turntable you may have to turn the food several times during cooking, to make sure it cooks evenly.

This book, like other microwave recipe books cannot always give you precise and accurate cooking times because these vary. Watch the food carefully as it nears the end of the cooking time, remembering that it will continue to cook after the oven is turned off.

Make a note of the time required, the dish used etc, so you have a guide the next time you use the same recipe.

When you can smell the food cooking in the microwave oven you know that it is nearly ready.

Don't Turn On An Empty Microwave

You should not turn on your microwave oven when it has nothing in it to absorb the microwave energy, because the magnetron may be damaged. (If there is any chance that your oven may be turned on in error, leave a glass of water in it.)

When you use a browning dish, however, you preheat the empty browning dish in an otherwise empty oven. The coating on the base of the dish absorbs the microwaves and heats up, heating the dish sufficiently to brown food.

Metal in Microwave Ovens

Microwaves cannot pass through metal. Small amounts of metal sometimes cause arcing, making sparks.
- Do not cook food in metal pots, pans, bowls etc.
- Do not leave metal spoons in cups or bowls.
- Do not seal ovenbags with metal-cored twist ties.
- Remove metal bag-sealing rings from frozen foods.
- Remove metal tops before microwaving jars of food.
- Do not cook or warm foods in china with gold or silver patterns on it.

In some microwave ovens you can use small amounts of metal — e.g. shallow foil dishes, metal racks etc. Different rules apply for different types of ovens, especially "combination" ovens. Follow the instructions in the manual which comes with your particular microwave oven.

Small amounts of aluminium foil, which stop parts of unevenly-shaped foods overcooking or defrosting too fast, are generally permitted.

Any metallic objects put in your oven should not touch the walls. Most metal meat thermometers are not suitable for microwave ovens. If you have one of these, insert it and read the temperature only when the oven is off.
Always follow your oven manufacturer's instructions.

Standing Time

Food continues to cook after it is taken out of a microwave oven. Eg. a potato keeps baking for 1-2 minutes.

A roast continues to cook, and its internal temperature rises, for 10-15 minutes after it is taken from the oven.

The appearance and texture of the food change during this time. . .
- cabbage softens and brightens
- hamburgers and chicken get browner
- cake surfaces dry out

- crumble toppings become crisper

If you wait until food looks and feels cooked before you take it from the oven, you may well find that it is overcooked after standing. If in doubt, undercook. Take food out after the recommended time. You can always put it back in the oven if it is still undercooked after standing. It is much harder to render first aid to overcooked food!

Cooking Times Vary

- Machines with different wattage cook at different rates. The higher the wattage, the faster the food will cook.
- The higher the power level, the quicker the cooking will be. A cake, for example, will take about twice as long to cook at 50% power as it does to cook at 100% power, other things being equal.
- Initial temperature is important. Food from the refrigerator takes longer to cook than food from a warm room.
- Large amounts of food take longer to cook than small amounts of the same food.
- Dense foods take longer to cook than porous, light food of the same size and shape.
- Small pieces of food cook more quickly than large pieces, so finely chopped food will cook faster than large chunks, even though the total weight is the same.
- Foods containing a lot of water cook faster than drier foods.
- Foods with a high fat content cook more quickly than those which contain little fat.
- Food which contains a high proportion of sugar will cook more quickly than food with less sugar.
- The shape of the container affects the cooking time, e.g. a cake in a ring-shaped mould will cook faster than a cake in a round pan.
- Food arranged so that it is the same distance from the centre of the turntable will cook more quickly.
- Food placed so the densest part is to the outside will cook faster.
- A solid item which is turned over part way through cooking will cook more quickly and evenly than an unturned one.

When the total cooking time is very

short, cooking food for a minute longer than necessary will mean it is overcooked.

Because foods continue to cook after they are taken from the oven, you should try to stop cooking them just before they are completely cooked.

What Do I Cook First?

If you are planning to cook most of a meal in your microwave oven, you should work out the cooking order carefully.
- First, cook foods that will be served cold.
- Next, cook foods that reheat easily.
- Then cook foods that will hold their heat and/or which require a long standing period.
- Last, cook food with short cooking times or foods which may overcook if reheated, such as eggs and fish.

Cook desserts first as they can easily be warmed up while the main course is being eaten.

Cook meat next. Meat usually holds its heat well and often requires standing time. If it does cool quickly, you will be able to reheat it quickly, too.

Cook vegetables after meat. Cook largest, densest vegetables (like baked potatoes) before shredded vegetables or vegetables like peas, which are in small pieces.

Sauces can be fitted in between other dishes, where suitable.

Bread rolls, etc. are usually reheated last, in their serving basket, lined with a napkin.

Do not plan to cook several containers of food at the same time, since it is hard to cook them evenly and estimate their cooking times. They are best cooked one after another. Although you can REHEAT combinations of food — i.e. a meal served on a plate — you get best results by heating or rewarming food in its serving dishes, then serving it on to individual plates.

Although microwave books often give elaborate timetables for cooking everything in the oven, it seems to me that it is more sensible to use the microwave and conventional oven or cook-top, side by side, when preparing dinners.

Find what pattern suits you best!

Microwaved Food May Look Different . . .

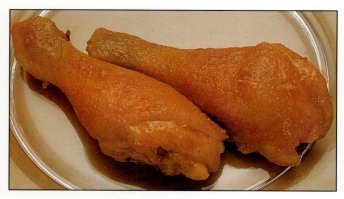

1. Fast cooking meats do not brown, but you can add toppings for colour as well as flavour before cooking them. Use commercial toppings or make your own.

2. Or you can cook them in the microwave, then brown them under the grill. You still save time, but you have the grill to clean later!

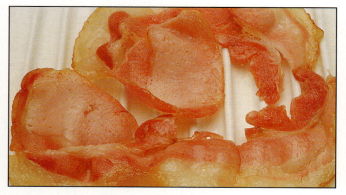

3. Colour sometimes improves during "standing time", e.g. a hamburger or meat loaf browns naturally after 3-4 minutes and a wholemeal loaf "crust" darkens and dries out after about an hour. Bacon darkens after 1-2 minutes.

4. You can add colour to cooked savoury foods by adding grated cheese, paprika, chopped parsley, or tomato ketchup after baking, before serving.

5. Chops, sausages, fish and steaks can be "seared" or browned in a preheated "browning dish" in the microwave oven at the start of their cooking time. This helps their texture, too.

6. Longer cooking meats that have a fat coating often brown normally as they cook. This lamb was roasted for about 15 minutes, with no additions.

. . . But You Can Easily Improve Its Appearance

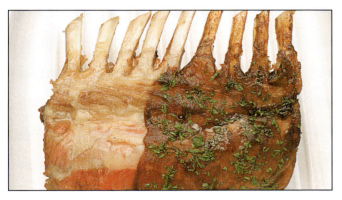

1. You can brush meat with soya sauce mixtures or gravy browning or dark powdered soup or sauce mixes before cooking to get a darker brown appearance.

2. You can add gravy browning to sauces or gravies which look too light coloured.

3. Baked plain mixtures look very pale. Sprinkle them with cheese, paprika, poppy seeds or sesame seeds before baking, or use browning spray. Top sweet mixtures with spice and sugar mixtures for browner, better appearance.

4. Ice cakes to hide their light top, or so that their "steamed" crustless surface will not be seen.

5. Use recipes containing cocoa, spices, brown sugar, golden syrup, malt or treacle, so colour is naturally rich and dark.

6. Create colourful toppings underneath the baked mixture, e.g. upside-down cake.

What Do You Cook In?

You will find that you will be able to cook in your microwave oven using many of the containers that you already have in your kitchen. As well as the paper items photographed, cardboard may be lined or covered with greaseproof paper and used as an oven-slide for biscuits, etc., or a cardboard box used as a cake pan when baking. Oven bags may be used for cooking, refrigerating, freezing and reheating food. They take up very little space in the refrigerator and may be re-used many times. Their rubber band (loose) fastening should be moved close to the food, so the food nearly fills the part of the bag used.

The plastic containers in which food is bought are useful, but tend to have a limited life. Heavier plastics, like jugs, may give good service for a long time. They have the advantage of lightness. Wooden spoons and stirrers may be left in mixtures which are stirred between periods of cooking. Wooden toothpicks and skewers are unaffected by microwaves. Shells make very good containers but may lose their natural gloss eventually.

Pottery containers which get warm when tested should not be used in the microwave. They have metallic substances in their body or glaze.

1. Paper plates, paper towels, paper napkins, paper cups, cup-cake liners and greaseproof paper may be used for warming, reheating, and cooking foods for short times. Cardboard boxes may be used, too.

3. Dishwasher-proof plastics are microwave-proof, too. Some plastics soften, distort and scar on prolonged heating with hot fats and sugary mixtures. Don't expect too much of them.

5. Many of the pottery and china containers from your cupboards may be used for microwave cooking and reheating as long as they do not have a metallic trim (gold or silver patterns).

2. Oven bags make excellent containers. Always leave a finger-sized gap and fasten with rubber bands. Many plastic bags melt if used with hot oils or sugar. Plastic cling wrap makes excellent covers.

4. Wood, cane and cloth may be microwaved for short times, when they are being used as food containers. Watch that no metal staples, etc. are used in their construction.

6. To test for microwave-proofness, stand a cup of water beside the container. Microwave on High for 1 minute. If water heats and container stays cool it can be used.

7. Use existing pyrex and other heat-resistant glass dishes for all cooking and heating. A large range is available, for microwave and regular oven use.

8. Inexpensive plastic mixing bowls make good, lightweight but tough microwave containers. They may scar with very hot fats and sugars.

9. When you are buying china, choose a type which may be microwaved. Some china may be used in conventional ovens, too.

What Do You Buy Especially?

1. Pyroceram (Corning Ware) and flame-resistant glass dishes have greatest versatility and may be used as containers for all household cooking. They often have lids.

3. Browning dishes have a special base which heats in an empty microwave, so dish acts as a frying pan, browning and crisping surface of food. Base gets very hot, so browners have legs.

5. Microwave muffin and cupcake pans may be used for eggs and for baking, with or without liners if they have solid bottoms. Alternately, cut paper cups to hold paper liners.

There is now a wide range of cooking utensils and dishes designed especially for microwave cooking. Often, prices give an indication of the quality and length of life of the product.

Pyroceram dishes and flame-resistant glass dishes may be used in nearly all cooking situations for microwaving, conventional baking, grilling, refrigeration, freezing, serving and stove-top cooking. Their only disadvantage is their weight. They stand temperature extremes but should still be cooled gradually.

Very few people will find they need a huge range of special-purpose dishes and prefer to use alternatives, until they know what foods they like microwaved. However, the use of some special purpose dishes will increase the range of foods microwaved and will often mean that foods can be cooked better, more evenly and with less fuss.

Covered dishes are especially useful, (though alternative covers may be used). Some dishes have covers which are intended for storage rather than microwaving or dishwashing. Check carefully before use, or you may distort them. A browning dish is invaluable to some people. Others prefer to microwave vegetables while they cook the meat, etc in a pan. Similarly meat thermometers, marvellously useful to some people, are unimportant for people who microwave chickens, but cook other roasts conventionally. When storage space and money are limited, invest in dishes which have many uses, and which are the right size for the foods you cook.

2. Roasting racks cook meat faster and more evenly. Fats and cooking liquids slow down cooking. Alternatively, invert a saucer, etc. on a dinner plate.

4. Microwave meat thermometers help you produce roasts cooked exactly as you like them. Alternatively, regular meat thermometers may be inserted at intervals while oven is not turned on.

6. My most used dish is light, has a cover, and is virtually unbreakable, with an optional cone for baking. It is made of T.P.X. and resists higher heat than other plastics. It may be used in a conventional oven.

7. Oven-proof glass measuring cups and bowls are useful for measuring and cooking foods which need stirring. Handles stay cool.

8. Stirrers and tongs made of tough heat-resistant plastic may be left in dishes in oven during cooking. Alternatively, use wooden spoons or remove metal utensils during cooking.

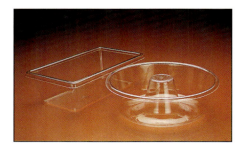

9. Relatively inexpensive plastic designed for microwave cooking is light and hard-wearing. Hot oil and melted sugar may melt some plastics. Alternatively, for ring pans, invert a jar or glass.

For Even Cooking

1. Cover or wrap food to spread heat evenly and to help food cook faster.

There are several easy ways in which you can ensure that the food in your microwave oven cooks as evenly as possible. Experiment to see what gives you best results in your particular oven.

Food which is cut into small pieces cooks more evenly than large pieces.

Change techniques where necessary. Cakes, uncovered conventionally, microwave better when covered.

Use ring pans when baking and at other times when centre food cooks more slowly.

Don't forget standing time! Heat spreads to central areas during this time where they will cook more slowly.

Arrange food carefully on turntable. Put one item in the centre. Space several items evenly, the same distance from each other and the centre. Arrange small items in a circle, without letting them touch each other.

2. Arrange food so thicker pieces are nearer the edge of the dish and the edge of the turntable.

3. Move food from the centre to the outside of container, part way through cooking. Stir, whisk, shake dish, etc.

4. Shield corners for whole or part of cooking when you cannot easily cover dish or stir it while it cooks.

5. Arrange delicate quick-cooking parts of food close to the centre where they will cook more slowly.

6. Turn and rearrange large pieces at least once during cooking.

7. Lift food from bottom of oven, using a roasting rack, an inverted plate, etc. Experiment with different heights.

Covers help Food Cook Faster and More Evenly

1. Paper towel wrappings spread heat, absorb some moisture and prevent baked food from becoming soggy.

2. A paper towel tent over meat prevents spattering, helps cook it evenly, and prevents steamed surface appearance.

3. Greaseproof paper holds more steam than paper towels. Quick-cooking vegetables for 1 serving may be wrapped in package of two layers of this.

4. Greaseproof paper "lid" over cake during baking prevents sticky undercooked surface spots, and helps cake rise evenly at high power levels.

5. Casseroles with close fitting lids keep steam around vegetables and many other foods during cooking and reheating. Open lid carefully to avoid steam burns.

6. Put a sheet of greaseproof paper under loose fitting casserole lid. (Loose fitting lid stops boilovers when cooking rice, etc.)

7. Plastic cling wrap keeps steam enclosed. Vent one side or pierce so film will not bubble up during cooking and suck down during cooling of food.

8. Oven bags loosely closed with rubber bands hold steam well, are reusable many times and may be adjusted to hold small or large amounts. Open bags with care.

9. To reheat several foods on same plate, cover fairly tightly. Use inverted pie plate or plate covers. If food is dryish, before covering sprinkle with water for extra steam.

10. Disposable showercaps and oven bags make reusable plate covers. Cling wrap may melt if it touches high fat, high sugar foods.

11. Plastic bags may be used for brief cooking or rewarming where sugars and fats do not raise temperature too high. They often melt.

12. Foods surrounded by thin skins and membranes do not need further covers to keep steam in. Pierce or cut skins to prevent steam build ups and explosions.

Reheating Cooked Food

Reheating is one of the most useful functions of a microwave oven.

It is important to reheat the food to exactly the right temperature — underwarmed food will have cold patches. Overwarmed food will overcook and will spoil. Baked products will dry out and toughen, especially if not eaten immediately. Dried out meats will shrink, toughen and lose liquid.

Plated meals require special thought.

If you are planning to reheat these later, arrange the food on the plate with care.

Put hard-to-heat foods close to the edge of the plate. Arrange food in a ring on the plate, leaving the centre relatively clear. Do not pile hard-to-heat food too high.

Mashed potato may be plated with a depression in the centre and have a small amount of butter added, to attract microwave energy. Dip sliced meat in gravy before arranging on plate. Do not pile too many slices on each other.

Experiment to see whether food reheats better in your oven if it is raised from the bottom, by standing it on an inverted plate.

1. Reheat individual portions rather than reheating a whole block of food, then cutting it up.

2. Reheat until bottom centre of plate feels warm.

3. Stand crisp foods on a ridged surface so no large part of them is lying on another surface.

4. Stir foods whenever possible, taking food from centre of dish to the edge.

5. Stand wedges of pie, etc. on several layers of paper towel. This will support the bottom of pie and will absorb moisture.

6. Covered food reheats faster. Sprinkle food with a few drops of water for extra steam for faster reheating.

7. Remove foods from foil dishes before reheating. Foil slows down reheating, even if "permitted" in your oven.

8. Lower power levels when food must be reheated as a large solid piece and cannot be stirred.

9. Read microwaving instructions on containers of ready cooked, reheatable foods.

10. Wrap foods which may get soggy on bottoms in paper towels. Take care not to overheat them.

Defrosting Frozen Food

1. Cover food during defrosting. Use oven bags, greaseproof paper or cling film if necessary. Stir free-flow food as it thaws, bringing centre food to sides.

3. Flex blocks of food as they defrost. This spreads defrosting and makes it more even.

Microwave defrosting is very fast and efficient. It is especially useful for blocks of dense food, e.g. roasts of meat which will thaw in a fraction of the time needed at room temperature. Read instruction book guide for defrosting times, and check food carefully as it defrosts. Alter times when necessary. Although you can defrost at any power level, low power levels of 20% and 30% produce best results with no parts starting to heat and cook while other parts are still frozen.

Standing time is important in defrosting. Thawing continues during this time.

Although frozen vegetables may be cooked without defrosting, other foods, like meat and poultry, cook unevenly and are sometimes tougher if not defrosted at low power levels before cooking. These rules apply during manual thawing. Use your oven manufacturer's instructions for automatic defrosting.

2. When home freezing, freeze food in blocks which will thaw fast. Wrap or pack in microwave-proof containers.

4. When thawing a block of minced meat, scrape off and remove outer thawed portion so it does not overheat while centre part is still frozen.

5. Remove ice crystals from baked products before thawing, since these cause sogginess.

6. Pour off liquid from defrosting food at intervals, so still-frozen food will thaw more quickly.

7. Remove frozen foods from metal TV dinner trays. Arrange it on plate with slow-thawing foods closest to edge of plate. Cover plate before defrosting.

8. As large items start to thaw, turn them and cover thin sections with small pieces of foil to stop them cooking before main part defrosts.

9. To thaw half (or more) of a large item, cover rest with foil. Shielded portion will not thaw and may be refrozen when thawed section is removed.

10. Always remove metal-cored twist ties and other metal bag fasteners before thawing. These may cause arcing and make sparks.

Spectacular And Easy . . .

MAKE DRINKS IN MUGS AND CUPS. Boil water in a mug or cup, then add a teabag or a spoonful of instant coffee. Fill with tap water and heat to drinking temperature. You can reheat a drink which has cooled down, taking care not to overheat and let it boil. Time will vary with cup size and temperature, from 1-3 minutes.

MAKE A MUG OF HOT CHOCOLATE. Put drinking chocolate, Milo etc in mug with (water and) milk, using proportions to suit yourself. Microwave, uncovered, on High (100% power) for 1½-2 minutes, to desired heat. Stir and add marshmallow for last 20 seconds, if desired.

MAKE HOT CHEESY SAVOURIES. Arrange crackers in a circle on a flat, round plate (with no metallic trim). Spread with grated or sliced cheddar or processed cheese, pieces of bacon or salami, pieces of gherkin, sliced mushrooms, etc. Heat, uncovered, on High (100% power) until cheese melts, for 1-3 minutes, depending on the size, number, etc. Serve 1-2 minutes after cooked.

MAKE CHEESE ON TOAST. If you want extra flavour and colour, spread toast with pickle, chutney, sliced tomatoes, etc. Slice fairly soft or processed cheese and lay on toast, leaving space for spreading at edges. Place on paper towel and microwave on High (100% power) for 30-75 seconds, or until cheese melts.

MAKE HOT DOGS. Put saveloy or frankfurter in a buttered split bun, adding mustard, relish, tomato sauce, etc. Wrap in a paper towel. Microwave on High (100% power) for 45 seconds to 1 minute.

HEAT SPAGHETTI ON TOAST. Open a tin of spaghetti or baked beans and spoon half a cup onto a piece of buttered toast on a plate (without metallic trim). Cover plate loosely with greaseproof paper. Microwave on High (100% power) for about 1½ minutes.

COOK BACON. Place a rasher on individual serving plate without metallic trim. Cover lightly with paper towel. Microwave on High (100% power) for 1-1½ minutes until bacon looks nearly cooked. (It will brown on standing). Turn halved tomatoes (or mushrooms) in bacon fat. Cover again. Cook 30-45 seconds, until tender.

MAKE SCRAMBLED EGGS. Mix 1 egg with 2 tablespoons milk and a pinch of salt in a pyrex measuring cup or small bowl, using a fork. Microwave on High (100% power) for 30 seconds, stir, then cook about 30 seconds more, until volume increases. Stir gently. Leave to stand for 1 minute to finish cooking. If not firm enough, heat a little longer.

COOK CORN ON THE COB. Put corn cob (exactly as picked) in microwave oven with no wrapping, coating or additions. Microwave on High (100% power) for about 3 minutes. Leave for 1 minute. Cut through stem end to detach all outer layers. Peel away outer layers and silk. Add butter and eat immediately.

BAKE A POTATO. Scrub an evenly shaped potato. Pierce in several places. Microwave on High (100% power) for 3-5 minutes, until potato "gives" when pressed. Turn potato upside down after 2 minutes for even cooking. (Potato continues cooking during 3-4 minutes standing time.)

MAKE PORRIDGE IN A BOWL. Put ¼ cup rolled oats in a fairly small porridge bowl. Add ½ cup hot tap water and pinch of salt.
Microwave, uncovered, on High (100% power) for 1½ minutes, stirring once during cooking and as soon as cooking has finished. (For variations, see page 100)

WATCH POPPADOMS RISE, WRINKLE AND COOK LIKE MAGIC! Put 1 large or 2 small poppadoms, straight from their packet, on a paper towel, microwave uncovered on High (100% power) for 45 seconds to 1 minute, until whole surface buckles. Remove before it browns and leave 30 seconds. Whole surface should be crisp. Adjust times, if necessary. Serve as snacks with dips or soups.

Microwave Tips — Ways With Bread

TO MAKE CROUTONS. Melt 2 Tbsp butter in a flat-bottomed dish on High (100% power) for 45 seconds. Toss with 1 cup of small bread cubes. Sprinkle with ¼ tsp garlic salt. Add paprika and curry powder if desired. Microwave uncovered, on High (100% power) 3-4 minutes, stirring after 2 minutes until slightly browned. Stand 5 minutes on paper towel to crisp.

FOR CRISP BREAD SLICES. Warm 2 Tbsp butter with ¼ tsp garlic salt and ⅛ tsp paprika to easy spreading consistency, 20-30 seconds on High (100% power). Mix well, then spread on 12-16 slices of French bread or on 4 quartered slices of bread. Arrange on a ridged roasting pan or on paper towels. Allow about 15 seconds per slice or piece.

SAVOURY CRUMBS FOR TOPPINGS AND COATINGS. Melt 1 Tbsp butter in flat-bottomed dish on High (100% power) for 30 seconds. Toss with 2 cups fresh breadcrumbs, stirring frequently when crumbs start to change colour (2-4 minutes).
FOR HERBED CRUMBS Add 1-2 Tbsp parsley or other herbs to uncooked buttered crumbs.

FOR BARBECUE BREAD. Mix 50g soft butter, 1 cup grated cheese, 2 chopped spring onions, 2 finely chopped garlic cloves and 2 Tbsp tomato concentrate. Cut French bread in slices to within 5mm of bottom crust. Spread seasoned mixture on each slice. Wrap bread in paper towel. Microwave on High (100% power) until cheese melts and bread is warm.

WARMING BREAD IN BASKET. Place sliced French bread, rolls, croissants, muffins, etc. in a napkin-lined basket and microwave on High (100% power) until outside of bread feels slightly warm. Six rolls will take about 15 seconds, 10 rolls, about 30 seconds. Do not overheat. Centre of bread is always hotter than the crust.

TO FRESHEN BREAD, MUFFINS, CAKE AND PITA BREAD. Put the bread, etc. in a roasting bag and microwave on High (100% power) for 10-30 seconds. Serve immediately.

Microwave Tips — For Chocolate And Babies

TO MELT CHOCOLATE. Break into small pieces or put chocolate morsels in a small round bowl. Microwave on High (100% power), checking every 30 seconds until it melts when stirred. (Chocolate will keep its shape until touched, even when melted). Do not heat longer than necessary. ½ cup morsels melt after 1-1½ minutes.

FOR CHOCOLATE WRITING OR DECORATIONS. Place ¼ cup chocolate morsels in a small plastic bag flat on a paper towel. Microwave on High (100% power) until chocolate melts, about 1 minute. Press bag to make sure chocolate is completely melted. Snip a small hole in corner. Squeeze folded bag, adjusting the flow of chocolate.

TO MAKE CHOCOLATE ICING: Put ½ cup of chocolate morsels in a bowl, microwave on High (100% power) for 2-3 minutes, until melted. Stir in ¼ cup sour cream. Sufficient to ice sides and top of a 23cm round cake. (Refrigerator cake after icing.)

FOR A CHILD'S BISCUIT SANDWICH. Place a fairly plain sweet biscuit or cream cracker on a folded paper napkin or towel. Top with 4-6 chocolate morsels and a marshmallow. Microwave on High (100% power) until marshmallow puffs up and chocolate melts, 20-30 seconds. Top with another biscuit.

HEATING A BABY'S BOTTLE. Place bottle of baby's milk, with or without the teat, with plastic top loosely screwed, in microwave oven. Heat on High (100% power) for 20-50 seconds, depending on the amount of milk and its initial temperature. ALWAYS shake bottle and test temperature on your wrist before giving it to a baby.

TO WARM BABY FOOD. Microwave plate of cooked or prepared food, uncovered, on High (100% power) allowing about 15 seconds per 2 tablespoons of food. To thaw and reheat cubes of frozen vegetables, etc. microwave on High allowing about 2 minutes per cube. Stir as soon as food has thawed. ALWAYS check heat of food by tasting it yourself before feeding it to a baby or toddler.

TO SOFTEN BUTTER FOR THE TABLE. Place about 100g unwrapped butter from refrigerator on a butter dish without metallic trim.
Microwave on Medium (50% power) for 10-15 seconds or until slightly soft. Butter will soften more on standing.

TO SOFTEN CREAM CHEESE FOR SPREADING OR MIXING. Place a small amount of cream cheese into a small dish. Cover with waxed paper and microwave on Medium (50% power) for ½-1 minute. (A 225g carton will take 1½-2 minutes on Medium (50% power) or 45-60 seconds on High (100% power).

TO SOFTEN OR LIQUIFY HONEY, SYRUP, OIL OR SALAD DRESSING. Microwave on High (100% power) for 30-45 seconds or until desired consistency is obtained. (If warming honey, etc. in its jar, be sure to remove metal lid.)

WARM BRIE OR CAMEMBERT CHEESES to good serving temperature instantly, instead of leaving them at room temperature for 24 hours, etc. Unwrap cheese, place on board. Heat a 125g cheese at Medium-high (70% power) for 30-45 seconds, until slightly warmed right through.

OPEN SHELLFISH EASILY. Arrange oysters in shells in a circle in a shallow covered casserole. Microwave on High (100% power). Start with 5 seconds per shellfish. Remove as soon as each opens slightly. Insert knife to cut muscle. For mussels or cooked shellfish, allow longer time, until shell can be removed without cutting. DO NOT OVERCOOK.

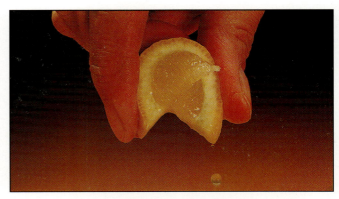

FOR MORE JUICE FROM CITRUS FRUIT. Microwave on High (100% power) for about 30 seconds. Let the fruit stand for about 3 minutes and roll it between your hands or on a board several times before cutting and squeezing.

Microwave Tips — Snacks

ROASTING NUTS. Lightly brown 1 cup nuts and 1 tsp oil on High (100% power) for 6 minutes or until golden. For savoury nuts, after roasting, mix in ½ tsp worcestershire sauce, ½ tsp garlic salt, and a few drops of hot pepper sauce. Microwave 1 minute.

TO MAKE QUICK NACHOS. Spread 20-30 corn chips on a paper (or ordinary) plate. Cover with a layer of grated cheese (about 1 cup). Sprinkle with seasoning mixture made by mixing ½ tsp hot pepper sauce, ½ tsp salt, 1 tsp mild vinegar and 1 tsp water. Microwave on Medium (50% power) 1½-3 minutes, until cheese melts.

RECRISP SOFTENED POTATO CHIPS, NUTS, POPCORN, CRACKERS, ETC. Lay them on several layers of paper towels (preferably on a ridged roasting pan.) Microwave on High (100% power) until food feels warm, starting with 20 seconds. Cool before serving.

TO TOAST SESAME SEEDS. Microwave 1 Tbsp butter in a small dish on High (100% power) for 40 seconds or until melted. Add ¼ cup sesame seeds, stirring each minute until the seeds are light brown. Seeds in centre of dish brown first. Drain on a paper towel.

REHEAT PRECOOKED FOODS IN THE CONTAINER IN WHICH THEY WILL BE SERVED. Heat pre-cooked foods on High (100% power). Remember that eating temperature is usually less than boiling. Stir foods several times for even reheating. Leave liquid foods uncovered but cover drier foods.

TO MAKE QUICK SOUP. In a mug or bowl measure concentrated canned soup, add same amount of hot tapwater and heat 2-3 minutes on High (100% power). For instant packet soup boil water in mug or bowl, then stir in packet contents. Reheat briefly if desired.

Microwave Tips — Vegetables, Sauce And Meat

MAKE INSTANT SAUCE, GRAVY OR SOUP. Use a measuring cup or mug and follow packet instructions. For maximum thickening, microwave on High (100% power) for 1-2 minutes, or until soup bubbles vigorously around the edge. Stir well. Reheat in same container if not all required immediately, adding a little extra liquid if needed.

BAKE TOMATOES EASILY. Halve or thickly slice tomatoes and season to taste or cut a deep cross in the top of whole tomatoes to prevent steam build up. Cook uncovered until soft on High (100% power) allowing 30-60 seconds per tomato.

TO CUT PUMPKIN MORE EASILY. Soften pumpkin, butternuts, etc. by first microwaving them uncovered on High (100% power) for 1-2 minutes. Let stand for 1-2 minutes before cutting.

TO PRE-COOK POTATOES. (For 600-800g potatoes). Peel and halve potatoes. Place in an oven bag with ¼ cup water. Close loosely with a rubber band, leaving a finger-sized hole. Microwave on High (100% power) for 6-8 minutes, until just cooked. Brown in roasting pan in conventional oven; in oil in frying pan; or roughen skin, brush with oil and brown under grill.

TO FINISH COOKING PREVIOUSLY BROWNED FOOD. After browning outer surfaces of food very quickly on barbecue, in frying pan or under grill, cool and refrigerate up to 1-2 days. Then finish cooking and reheat in the microwave oven. e.g. It takes 10-12 seconds on High (100% power) for a pre-browned 25g well-trimmed lamb cutlet.

SPEED UP BARBECUE COOKING (OR GRILLS). Microwave chicken or sausages without coatings until partly or nearly cooked. Then brush with glaze, barbecue sauce, etc. and brown close to heat.

Microwave Tips — For Easier Desserts

DISSOLVE GELATINE. Sprinkle gelatine over cold water or juice as required in recipe. Leave to stand 3 minutes. Heat on High (100% power) in 10 seconds bursts until gelatine has dissolved, stirring thoroughly between each heating. Time will vary with amount of liquid. Do not overheat.

STEWING DRIED FRUIT. Cover fruit with water, heat in covered dish on High (100% power) for 6-8 minutes. Stand, covered, 5 minutes, then add sugar to taste.

TO SOFTEN ICE CREAM. Place container of ice cream in the oven. Microwave on Medium (50% power) for 45 seconds to 1 minute. Let the ice cream stand 2-3 minutes before serving.

ROLLING FROZEN OR REFRIGERATED CREPES EASILY. Wrap the number of crepes needed in a paper towel. Microwave on High (100% power) approximately 4-5 seconds per crepe, until soft enough to roll easily without cracking or sticking. Warm sliced bread for asparagus or cheese rolls in the same way.

WARMING BRANDY FOR FLAMBÉ To warm brandy or other spirits before flaming them, heat on High (100% power) allowing 20 seconds for 2 tablespoons, then pour over food and light. (Warm brandy slightly before drinking it too, if desired.)

HEATING JAM FOR GLAZE AND SAUCES. Microwave jam in its jar if less than half full, or put the needed quantity into a small dish, allowing space for bubbling. Microwave on High (100% power) until jam melts. Stir every minute. Freshen opened jam the same way, adding extra liquid if necessary.

Microwave Tips — For Baking

TO SOFTEN BUTTER AND SUGAR FOR BAKING. Place the sugar and butter in a bowl and microwave on High (100% power) for 15-30 second intervals until butter is soft enough to cream. Do not overheat and melt butter.

TO SOFTEN HARD BROWN SUGAR. Into the bag of hardened sugar place a few drops of water or an apple wedge. Microwave on High (100% power) for 1½-2 minutes or until lumps soften. Let the sugar stand for 5 minutes.

PLUMP DRIED FRUIT FOR BAKING. Wash loose-packed dried fruit to remove any dirt or grit. Drain. Spread on several layers of paper towels on flat microwave dish. Microwave on High (100% power) until fruit is hot and surface dry. Allow to cool before using in baking.

TO BLANCH ALMONDS. Microwave ½ cup water in dish on High (100% power) for 1 minute or until boiling. Add ½ cup almonds (without shells) and microwave uncovered for 1 minute. Drain, pinch off skins, and dry on paper towels. To toast ¼ cup slivered almonds, turn in 1 tablespoon melted butter for 3 minutes or until straw coloured.

WARM FLOUR FOR BREADMAKING. When you are making bread, it is important to keep the ingredients at blood heat so the yeast will work properly. To warm the flour before it is stirred into the other ingredients, heat it on High (100% power) in 10 second bursts, until it feels warm. 1 cup flour requires 10-20 seconds.

RISE DOUGH FOR YEAST BREADS. If dough is kept at blood heat, it will rise quickly. Dough may be microwaved before it is shaped and after shaping. Rise dough in a covered container in the microwave oven on Defrost (30% power) for 1 minute at 5-10 minute intervals (for 1 loaf). Feel temperature of dough before and after microwaving.

FRESHEN AND PLUMP DRIED OR CRYSTALLISED FRUIT WHICH IS TO BE EATEN "AS IS". Rinse one fruit or a mixture. Spread on plate from which it will be served, cover and microwave on High (100% power) until fruit is hot. Leave to stand, covered, for 5 minutes, then uncover.

SAVE FIDDLY "LAST MINUTE" WORK WITH PLATED MEALS. Coat food with sauce, etc, and arrange one or more foods on individual plates or on a larger platter for "at table" service. Cover and reheat just before required on High (100% power) or on Medium-High (70% power) until centre of underside of plate feels hot.

TO WARM PLATES. Put 2 teaspoons of water on each plate, stack up and heat on High (100% power) 20-30 seconds per plate, or until hot.

FOR WARM, WET HAND TOWELS. After eating finger food, wet cloths and wring out the extra water. Roll each one and microwave on High (100% power) on a plate or basket, allowing about 30 seconds per towel.

TO MAKE INSTANT POT POURRI. Mix ½ cup scented flower petals or leaves with 1 tsp orris root. Dry between 2 folded paper towels until petals feel dry but still flexible, and leaves are crisp. Add spices, citrus rind etc. Store in shallow bowl, turning often, for 2-3 weeks, before covering.

DRY SMALL QUANTITY OF HERBS. Strip leaves from stems of clean, unwashed herbs like parsley, marjoram, thyme or mint and spread in a single layer between two folded paper towels. Microwave on high (100% power) until leaves are dry enough to crumble. (Overcooked leaves may brown). Time varies with the herb used. When cold, store in dark, airtight jars.

Light Meals

Light Meals

A microwave oven is marvellous for cooking snacks and light meals! Many mothers will find that children who would not take the time to cook themselves meals using a conventional stove, are very happy to prepare easy microwaved food, at all times of the day and night.

Cheese microwaves particularly well and forms an important part of quite a number of the recipes in this section.

You can make Macaroni Cheese using only one cooking container. Microwaved Cheese Fondue is foolproof!

Some egg recipes need lower power levels and careful timing, and are not suitable for beginners, but microwaved Scrambled Eggs can be made by a novice!

Do not try to boil or hardboil eggs in a microwave oven, but by all means use conventionally cooked eggs to make wonderfully easy Scotch Eggs!

Bread-based microwaved savouries are microwave stars! Adolescents and younger children love them, and can make them very easily! If you haven't tried heating a slice of cold cooked meat, moistened with gravy, dressing or chutney, in a split roll or sandwich, I hope you will try it soon. Hot sandwiches like these make excellent use of leftover cooked meat.

Pâtés and terrines cook quickly and easily too. They make good snack foods, but elegant meal starters, too. It pays to keep packets of chicken livers in the freezer, so these can be made and served at short notice.

In the same way, the little meat balls in this section may be cooked or reheated for a light meal, but can also be coated with well seasoned microwave sauces and passed round with drinks.

It is easy to make a quick pizza from basic ingredients if you have a browning dish. If not, just pile the topping on bread that is already cooked.

Last in this section is a savoury flan. Using this recipe as a guide, you will be able to modify your favourite savoury pie recipes, if you feel inclined!

Make sure that everyone in your household learns to cook the simple recipes in this section!

Macaroni Cheese

This recipe needs no draining and uses only one dish. For a crisp topping, sprinkle cooked mixture with Savoury Crumbs or crushed potato crisps before serving.

For 4 servings:
100g butter
about 2 cups (200g) macaroni, kiferi, lisci or perciatelli
1 tsp garlic salt
3 cups boiling water
3 cups grated cheese
3 Tbsp flour

In a large, 8-10 cup casserole (to prevent boil-overs) heat the butter on High (100% power) for 1½ minutes or until it melts. Stir in the macaroni and garlic salt. Pour boiling water over macaroni. Microwave, uncovered, for 12-15 minutes or until macaroni is tender, and most of the water absorbed. Mix the grated cheese with the flour. Stir into macaroni. Heat until cheese melts and mixture bubbles around the edges. If mixture is too thick, stir in a little milk and reheat till bubbling again.
Note: Use any pasta shapes, allowing a little longer for larger, thicker ones.

Cheddar Cheese Fondue

2 cups grated cheddar cheese (150g)
2 Tbsp flour
1 clove garlic, chopped
½ tsp nutmeg
1 cup flat or fresh beer

Mix grated cheese and flour in a bowl or flat-bottomed casserole dish. Add garlic, nutmeg and beer. Stir to mix. Heat on High (100% power) for 2 minutes, stir (with a whisk, if possible). Heat for another 2 minutes or until whole surface bubbles, stirring after each minute. Serve hot, reheating fondue when it becomes cool. To serve, dip crusty bread, apple or pear wedges, or raw cauliflower into hot fondue.

Microwaved Eggs

Scrambled eggs cook very easily and quickly, but you may need to experiment a little before you can cook perfect poached or fried eggs. You will need to find the right power level, plate and covering before you get both the white and yolk cooked exactly as you want them.

At high power levels the yolk tends to cook before the white close to it. It is a good idea to prick egg yolks with a skewer before cooking, to save spattering and mini-explosions. Do not cook eggs in their shells in the microwave oven. As the yolk goes from soft to hard boiled, it expands and the egg may explode. You can hard-cook a poached egg easily, however.

Scrambled Eggs

Cook scrambled eggs in pyrex measuring cups or bowls, or cook one or two scrambled eggs in a small bowl from which they may be eaten.

For 1 egg, melt a teaspoon of butter in a measuring cup. Add 2 tablespoons of milk, some finely chopped parsley or chives (if you like them), break in the egg, and mix with a fork until combined.

Microwave on High (100% power) for 30-40 seconds, stir to move the cooked egg to the centre, then cook for about 30 seconds longer, until you see the egg increase in volume. Remove, stir gently, then leave to stand for about a minute, to finish cooking. If the egg is not firm enough, heat again, in 10 or 20 second bursts.

2 eggs and ¼ cup milk cook in about 2-3 minutes.
4 eggs and ½ cup milk cook in about 4 minutes.
Note: Leave out butter, if preferred. Add a pinch of salt.

Poached Eggs

Microwaved poached eggs cook fastest in custard cups or in measuring cups, where ¼ cup of water will cover the egg as it cooks. When more water is used, the cooking time increases.

Pour ¼ cup boiling water into a measuring cup (or bring cold water to the boil). Slip the egg into the boiling water. Stab the yolk several times.

Cook on Medium (50% power) for about 1 minute or on Defrost (30% power) for 1¼-1½ minutes. Leave to stand for 30 seconds.

For a hard-yolked poached egg instead of a hard boiled egg, follow the previous instructions, but cook for 2 minutes on Medium (50% power) or 2½-3 minutes on Defrost.

For 2 poached eggs, use ½ cup boiling water and allow about 2½ minutes on Medium or 3-4 minutes on Defrost.

Baked Eggs

Serve each egg in its own little ramekin, on a plate with toast fingers for dipping.

Melt 1 teaspoon of butter on High (100% power) for 20 seconds. Break egg into butter. Sprinkle with 1 Tablespoon finely grated cheese, some parsley, spring onion or chives, and a pinch of paprika. Prick yolk several times. Bake, uncovered, on Medium (50% power) for 1½ minutes.
Variation: Cover and cook slightly shorter time, if preferred.

Bacon and Eggs

This may require a little practice! You can cook bacon and eggs on an ordinary plate, as long as its sides curve up so they are higher than the yolk. For ease, you may decide to use a plate with higher sides (see photograph).

Put a rasher of bacon on the plate. Depending on the size and thickness of the bacon, microwave on High (100% power) for 1-2½ minutes, until nearly cooked.

Turn a few small mushrooms in the bacon fat if desired. Push to the side of the dish. Break in the egg, so its yolk is in the centre of the plate. Add 1 small halved tomato if you like. Prick the egg yolk several times.
Cover plate with cling wrap. Microwave at Defrost (30% power). Set time for 3 minutes, but look at egg every 30 seconds after 2 minutes.

Turn off as soon as the egg white close to the yolk has set. The exact time will depend on the amount of bacon, mushroom and tomato, and the initial temperature and size of the egg.

Experiment with a cover made of a flat piece of greaseproof paper, and higher power levels. The egg will cook faster without tomato and mushrooms.

Bacon

Bacon microwaves superbly in a very short time. You can cook it on its serving plate, if you like. When cooking one or two rashers, lay them flat on a plate with a paper towel loosely over them to stop spatters.
1 rasher of bacon cooks on High (100% power) in about 1 minute — less if very thin — and up to 1½ minutes if large and thick.
Bacon browns and crisps on standing. Stop cooking it before it looks cooked.
For more slices, cook bacon on a dish with a ridged surface. Bacon will cook on both sides, out of fat.

Note: Cook only very fatty bacon between paper towels. Lean bacon sticks to them and cannot curl attractively as it cooks.

Cook bacon on a preheated browning dish if preferred. Preheat browning dish for 5-6 minutes. Immediately add bacon. Cook 30-45 seconds per rasher.

Scotch Eggs

Microwaved Scotch Eggs are marvellous. Try them!

For 4 servings:
1 cup soft breadcrumbs
1 Tbsp tomato sauce
2 tsp dark soy sauce
½ tsp curry powder
450-500g sausage meat
4 eggs, hard boiled
1 cup Savoury Crumbs
*   (see page 16) or dry breadcrumbs*

Combine first four ingredients with the sausage meat, mixing well. Divide the mixture into four equal parts. With wet hands, form the mixture around each egg, one at a time, cooking the first egg while coating the second, etc. Roll each coated egg in Savoury or dry breadcrumbs. Microwave each egg on High (100% power) for 2 minutes, or until coating is firm, turning after 1 minute. Cool. Halve or quarter the eggs just before serving at room temperature.

Quick Snacks and Savouries

With a microwave you can produce wonderful "instant" hot bread-based snacks, large or small, plain or fancy. For the bases use: bread rolls or hamburger buns, French bread halved lengthwise or cut into slices, English muffins, firm-textured plain or toasted bread slices, water biscuits or different types of crackers.

If you want crisp bases, you should toast bread products before filling or topping them. The microwave heats the bases, but it does not crisp them.

Use your imagination in creating the toppings. Look in your refrigerator or cupboard for all sorts of possible ingredients. Because cheese heats through very fast, it is nearly always included in fillings and toppings. It can be sliced, grated or chopped.

Cold meat and poultry make good fillings, too. When you include cooked meats in the filling, you should moisten them with gravy or chutney or relish, mild mixed mustard, tomato sauce or mayonnaise, whether the meat is left in slices or chopped.

Because the toppings and fillings do not brown as they heat, you should make sure you put some colourful items where they will show. If this is not possible, add a garnish after cooking. You can assemble snacks whenever it suits you, then heat them on their serving dish just before they are needed.

For interesting combinations, look through American cook books, reading the recipes for hot sandwiches, heros, sloppy Joes, etc.

It is a good idea to wrap sandwiches in paper towel parcels to hold them together and spread the heat evenly during heating.

Cooking times will vary with the size of the snack, its initial temperature, and its ingredients. Heat on High (100% power), watching ingredients carefully. Do not overheat, or bread will toughen and the cheese will spread everywhere.

For fillings, use:
sliced roast or corned beef, luncheon sausages or frankfurters, ham, bacon or salami, chicken or turkey, cooked sausages, scrambled eggs, tuna, salmon, sardines, cooked mince mixtures, mushrooms, tomatoes, radishes, red and green peppers, sauerkraut or pickled cabbage, gherkins or cucumber pickles, mustard pickles, pineapple or apple, spring onions or mild onions.

For moisteners use:
butter or mayonnaise
mixed mustard
tomato sauce
sour cream
relishes or chutney
canned spaghetti or baked beans

Hot Meat Sandwiches

A delicious way to use up leftover cold meat or poultry.

For 1-2 servings:
1 crusty bread roll
mayonnaise or butter
1-2 slices roast, corned beef, chicken or other cold meat
gravy (optional)
1 Tbsp mild mixed mustard
1 Tbsp relish or tomato sauce

Split the bread roll (not quite all the way through) and spread the cut surface with mayonnaise or butter. Slice, chop or fold the meat, adding a little leftover gravy, if desired. Place the meat in the roll. Add mustard and relish, tomato sauce, etc. Fold a paper towel around the roll and heat on High (100% power) for 30 seconds or until meat is hot and roll is warm.
Note: If meat is dry, spread with relish before placing in roll.

Stuffed Pita Bread

Change the filling to suit yourself, but include some meat or cheese.

For 4 servings:
2 large pita breads, halved
2 cloves garlic, crushed
2 Tbsp oil
1/2 tsp paprika
2 spring onions, sliced
2 cups chopped mushrooms
1/2 cup chopped ham or luncheon sausage
1/2 tsp dried basil
1/2 tsp dried oregano
1 Tbsp parmesan cheese
1/2 tsp salt
1 green pepper, chopped
2 tsp lemon juice
thin slices of tomato
lettuce leaves for garnish

Heat the garlic, oil and paprika on High (100% power) for 1½ minutes. Remove garlic and brush some of the oil on the outside of the pita bread. To the remaining oil add the spring onions, mushrooms, ham or sausage, herbs, cheese, salt, green pepper and lemon juice. Toss and stuff this mixture into the pita bread, placing the bread side by side in the serving basket so that the openings are facing upwards. Cover with cling wrap and heat on High for 2 minutes. Remove from oven. Remove cling wrap. Add slices of tomatoes and a few lettuce leaves to the top of the bread before

serving.
Note: Wrap individual "pockets" in cling wrap, if preferred. When required, heat each for 30 seconds. Unwrap and eat immediately.

Bread Roll Savouries

Good for lunch or a late night snack.

For 1 serving:
1 crusty bread roll, halved
1 onion, sliced
2 tsp oil
1/4 tsp paprika
4-6 slices cheese
4-6 flat anchovies
2-3 olives, sliced
fresh basil or parsley, chopped

Slice onion and mix in a bowl with the oil and paprika. Cover and microwave on High (100% power) for 1½ minutes. Brush the cut surface of the roll with a little of the oil mixture. Place each roll on a paper towel. Arrange cheese, anchovies, sliced onions and olives on the cut surface. Brush with the remaining oil. Heat 30 seconds to 1 minute until cheese melts and bread is warm.

Hot Bubbly Cheese Savouries

For 3-6 servings:
3 bread rolls, split (and toasted if desired)

2 eggs
1 rasher bacon, finely chopped
1 tomato, chopped
2 spring onions, chopped
1 cup grated cheese
paprika

With a fork, beat together the eggs, bacon pieces, chopped tomato, and onion. Put each of the bread roll halves on a paper towel and spread the cut side with the mixture. Add the cheese and sprinkle with paprika. Heat on High (100% power) for about 2 minutes or until cheese begins to bubble nicely.
Variation: Spread topping on toast, if preferred. Heat 2-3 slices at a time.

Hot Dogs

When you are serving a number of Hot Dogs, you can prepare them before you need them. Split each roll. Spread thinly with butter, then spread with tomato ketchup and mustard. Put frankfurter or saveloy in roll, adding other relish or a slice of cheese as well, if desired. Wrap each prepared Hot Dog in a paper towel. When required, cook each on High (100% power) for 45 seconds to 1 minute, until frankfurter is hot and roll warm. (Time the first frankfurter carefully, then heat the rest for the same time.)

Chicken Liver Savouries

Fast, tasty and inexpensive!
For 2-3 servings:
2 rashers bacon
2 Tbsp butter
2 cloves garlic, chopped
½ tsp chopped thyme
300g chicken livers
1 Tbsp flour
1 tsp chicken stock granules
2 tsp dark soya sauce
½ cup hot water
1 Tbsp sherry (optional)

Cook the bacon rashers on High (100% power) for 1½-2 minutes. Remove from dish and chop. To the dish add the butter, chopped garlic and thyme. Cut each chicken liver into four pieces and stir pieces into the butter mixture. Cover and cook 3-4 minutes, until livers are just firm. Stir in remaining ingredients, including the chopped bacon. Cover and cook 3 minutes more, or until liquid thickens. Taste, season and thin with extra liquid if necessary.
Variations: (a) Add 1 cup chopped mushrooms with chicken livers. (b) Cook 1 chopped apple in bacon fat before adding butter, etc.

Quick Kidneys

For 2-3 servings:
6 lambs' kidneys (about 300g)
2 rashers bacon (coarsely chopped)
1 Tbsp flour
¼ cup water
1 tsp dark soya sauce
¼ tsp salt
freshly ground black pepper

Halve, then slice kidneys, discarding all fat and membrane. Combine all of the ingredients in a bowl or casserole. Cover and microwave on High (100% power) for 6 minutes. Sprinkle with parsley. Serve on toast, rice, or noodles.

Country Terrine

This terrine cooks quickly and tastes excellent, but it is not an exciting mixture when it is raw!

300g cubed lamb's liver
1 egg
¼ cup sherry
1-2 garlic cloves
½ tsp salt
1 tsp fresh thyme
¼ tsp grated nutmeg
¼ tsp dried sage
⅛ tsp ground cloves
300g sausage meat
2-4 thin rashers bacon

Trim and cut liver into small cubes. Process until puréed, then add the egg, sherry and seasonings. Add sausage meat in several pieces, process until mixed. Line a microwave loaf pan with a long strip of ovenbag down its long sides and bottom. Arrange thin bacon strips on bottom. Pour the mixture evenly over this. Fold ends of ovenbag over meat. Stand loaf pan on an inverted plate. Microwave on Medium-high (70% power) for 6-7 minutes or until loaf springs back when pressed and juices from centre do not run pink. Lay something flat on terrine and weigh down with anything heavy, until cool. Unmould and slice.

Chicken Liver Pâté

This is a smooth, delicious pâté. For formal service, use individual pots. The glaze on top is pretty, but optional. For casual service, pour into a pottery bowl and cover to refrigerate.

400g chicken livers
¼ cup dry or medium sherry
1 Tbsp brandy (optional)
50g butter
1 clove garlic, chopped
1 Tbsp finely chopped onion
¾ tsp salt
1 Tbsp chopped parsley
½ tsp dried thyme
½ tsp dried marjoram

Thaw livers if necessary. Separate the two lobes of the livers, discarding fibrous portion. Halve each lobe. Add sherry and brandy. Leave to stand at least 5 minutes. Melt butter in fairly large microwave dish. Add remaining ingredients, then chicken livers and liquid. Cover. Microwave on High (100% power) for 4-5 minutes, until livers are pinkish grey, not red in centre when cut. Using metal chopping blade, process livers until smooth. Pour into one large or several small individual moulds.
Variation: Leave out sherry and brandy. Add 50g extra butter, 2 teaspoons worcestershire sauce and 1 teaspoon grated mace or nutmeg. Use fresh herbs, if possible.

For optional glaze:
1 tsp gelatine
½ cup cold water
½ tsp chicken stock granules
½ tsp dark soya sauce
bay leaves, green peppercorns, etc. for garnish (optional)

Soak gelatine in cold water, then heat with chicken granules and soya sauce. Pour over surface. Set bay leaves, etc. in glaze if desired.

Baby Meat Balls

Serve these with Barbecue or Spicy Indonesian Sauce as cocktail snacks.

For 4-6 servings:
250g minced lamb or beef
1 onion, chopped finely
1 cup soft breadcrumbs
½ tsp dried mint or basil
1½ tsp chicken stock granules
1 Tbsp lemon juice
1 tsp dark soya sauce

Thoroughly mix all ingredients in a food processor or bowl. With wet hands, shape the mixture into small balls (about 24). Arrange in a circle around the edge of the turntable or flat plate. Microwave, uncovered, on High (100% power) for 3-4 minutes or until firm. Brush with Spicy Indonesian Sauce or Barbecue Sauce and serve on toothpicks as cocktail savouries, or dilute either of the sauces with a little water in a casserole dish, add cooked meat balls, turning to coat, and serve with rice. Reheat meatballs when required.

Hot Barbecue Sauce

1 tsp chopped garlic
1 onion, chopped
1 Tbsp oil
2 Tbsp tomato ketchup
2 tsp tomato concentrate
1 Tbsp brown sugar
2 tsp worcestershire sauce
1 tsp mixed mustard

In a medium-sized bowl microwave garlic, onion and oil on High (100% power) for 3 minutes. Add the remaining ingredients and heat until mixture is bubbling (about 2 minutes). This sauce is especially good served on meatballs or frankfurters.

Spicy Indonesian Sauce

2 cloves garlic, chopped
2 tsp grated root ginger
1 tsp freshly ground coriander seed (optional)
2 Tbsp dark soya sauce
2 Tbsp lemon juice
1 Tbsp oil
3-4 drops hot pepper sauce
¼ cup brown sugar
2 Tbsp peanut butter
¼ cup water

Combine all the ingredients in a bowl and microwave, uncovered, on High (100% power) until smooth and thickened, about 4-5 minutes. Thin sauce with more water if necessary.

Pizza for Two

½ cup Alison Holst's Baking Mix
2-3 Tbsp milk
2 Tbsp oil
3 tomatoes, chopped
1 Tbsp tomato concentrate
½ tsp dried basil
½ tsp dried marjoram
1-1½ cup grated cheese
½-1 cup chopped mushrooms

Optional toppings: red and green peppers, sliced salami or bacon, black or green olives, anchovies, etc.

Put browning dish to heat for 6 minutes. Add enough milk to baking mix to make a fairly firm dough. Knead dough in bowl until smooth. On a board floured with additional mix, roll to 23cm round. Dampen edges with more milk and fold them over about 1cm, making a neat circular base. Brush top of dough with some of the oil. Prick in several places. Place the oiled side down in the heated browning dish and microwave on High (100% power) for 2 minutes or until firm enough to turn over. Turn and heat for 30 seconds longer. Mix tomatoes, concentrate, basil and marjoram and spread over the base, especially near the edge. Sprinkle with half of the cheese. Toss mushrooms and peppers in bowl with remaining oil and arrange them (and any additional toppings you like) over the cheese. Top with remaining cheese and heat until cheese melts, 2-4 minutes, depending on the amount of topping. Cut into slices and serve.

Salmon Flan

For 4-6 servings:
Pastry:
60-70g cold butter
1 cup flour
¼ tsp microwave browning liquid
4 Tbsp milk

Cut the cold butter into the flour until it resembles rolled oats. Add browning liquid to milk until medium-brown. Add this, a few drops at a time to flour, to form a stiff dough. Roll out very thinly. Drape over a 20-23cm inverted pie plate or casserole. Trim edges, moistening edge and folding it back if desired. Prick thoroughly. Microwave on High (100% power) for 5 minutes. If case tilts during cooking, reposition it. Cook until dry in centre. Turn right side up on serving plate. Pour prepared filling into cooked flan case. Cook on Medium (50% power) until just firm in centre, about 25 minutes. Remove from oven.

Filling:
1 cup cream
1 can (220g) salmon
paprika
¼ tsp salt
4 spring onions
4 eggs
1 cup grated cheese

In a medium-sized bowl, combine cream, undrained salmon, paprika, salt and spring onions. Heat until mixture bubbles around edge. Add eggs and grated cheese and beat with a fork until mixed. Spoon into cooked shell.

Soups

Soups

Microwaved soups? Most certainly! You will be amazed with the speed at which your microwaved soup will cook, and with its excellent fresh flavour.

The soups in this section are all quick, taking 15-40 minutes from start to finish. Although they can be eaten immediately, you will find that their flavour is even better if you make the soup ahead and re-heat it after it has stood for half an hour or more.

When you reheat soup in your microwave oven, you save dishwashing because the soup is in the mug or bowl from which you will eat it. None of your favourite, thick soups will scorch or stick to the bottom of their containers when microwaved, either.

To work most efficiently, use other appliances alongside your microwave oven when you make soup. Your food processor or blender will be invaluable for chopping vegetables and for puréeing many soups. You should heat water in your electric jug to thin down the thick microwaved mixtures in the following recipes. Most of the following recipes make 4-6 servings. Larger quantities take longer. Microwave soups often need less salt than regular soups. Many of these soups use "instant" stock granules. By all means replace instant granules and water with homemade or commercial stock, if you have it on hand. When you add stock granules, use restraint. More does not necessarily mean better. Always use level spoon measures. I find I get best flavour when I use small amounts, sometimes of several stocks-mixtures of chicken, beef and green herbs. Because these are salty, always taste before adding either seasoning.

For fastest soup-making use a large bowl-like container with fairly straight sides and a flattish bottom. You will need to cover many soups at the beginning of their cooking, so a lid is helpful. Use a container big enough to avoid boil-overs. (If you have a microwave oven with automatic functions, you will be able to reheat soup with even greater ease.) You may find a covered soup tureen a really practical investment. You can cook in it, reheat soup in it, and bring it to the table for dramatic presentation. Hunt in your bottom cupboards for a long forgotten tureen or see what you can find in second-hand shops.

Use your microwave oven for convenience soups, too. Dilute canned soup right in the mug or bowl. Add cold or boiling water to packet soups as instructed, and stir or whisk at intervals. Give make-in-a-mug instant soups a little extra heating after you add boiling water, as instructed.

Garnishes and Accompaniments
Take the time to garnish soups attractively, fitting the garnish to the soup. Use fresh herbs such as parsley, chives, spring onion, basil, dill, fennel and mint. Add colour with paprika, curry powder, grated nutmeg, etc. Reserve a little of one of the ingredients in a soup for garnish, e.g. vegetable slices, shrimps, shellfish, etc. Top with crisp bacon, sliced frankfurters or cooked sausages (sautéed or plain) or small dumplings. Add a spoonful or swirl of cream, sour cream or whipped cream.

Crisped breads of different types make good soup accompaniments, providing good texture contrast. e.g. make croutons (page 16), crisp bread slices (page 16), poppadoms (page 15). Buy potato crisps and corn chips for soup accompaniments, too. Serve freshly made toast or warm crusty bread rolls. Make the accompaniments substantial when soup is the main part of the meal. Keep them small and interesting when the soup is served as a meal starter.

Dumplings for Soup

½ cup self-rising flour
pinch of celery salt and garlic salt
1 Tbsp chopped parsley
other herbs to taste (optional)
¼ cup milk

Combine ingredients in order given, stirring just enough to dampen flour. Pour ½ cup hot water in a 23cm flat-bottomed dish. Drop mixture into water in about 12 small amounts, using two teaspoons. Cover. Cook on High (100% power) for 3 minutes, or until firm. Sprinkle with paprika if desired. Add to individual bowls of cooked soup.

Barley Broth

For 6-8 servings:
2 Tbsp butter
1 clove garlic, chopped
1 onion, chopped
1 carrot, grated or chopped
1 cup celery, sliced
¼ cup barley
1 Tbsp red lentils
1 Tbsp small yellow peas
4 cups boiling water
thyme, marjoram, basil
1 tsp chicken stock granules
1 tsp garlic salt
¼ cup chopped parsley

Heat butter, garlic, onion, carrot and celery in a large covered bowl or casserole on High (100%) power for 5 minutes, stirring once. Add barley, lentils, peas and 2 cups boiling water. Cover. Cook on medium (50% power) for 30 minutes. Add remaining boiling water, herbs to taste, stock granules, garlic salt and parsley, cook on Defrost, (30% power) for 10 minutes. Serve with Dumplings (see page 35).
Variation: Add 1-2 cups cooked chicken with the parsley.

Minestrone Soup

For about 8 servings:
2 Tbsp butter
1 onion, chopped
2 carrots, cubed
2 rashers bacon, chopped
3 cups boiling water
1 potato, cubed
¼ cup perciacelli
½-1 cup chopped zucchini
½-1 cup chopped green beans
1 cup chopped cabbage
1 (420g) can tomatoes in juice
1 can any coloured beans
2 tsp beef stock granules
1 tsp sugar

Combine first four ingredients in a large covered bowl or casserole. Microwave on High (100% power) for 4 minutes, stirring after 2 minutes. Add 1 cup boiling water, the potato and perciacelli. Stir, cover and cook 5 minutes longer. Add zucchini, beans, cabbage and tomato juice made up to 2 cup with boiling water. Cover and cook 5 minutes longer. Add chopped tomatoes, beans and the remaining 2 cups boiling water with the dissolved stock granules and sugar. Leave to stand until required. Heat until soup bubbles, stirring several times for even heating. Serve with parmesan cheese if desired.

Corn Chowder

For 4 servings:

2 Tbsp butter
1 large onion, chopped
2 stalks celery, sliced
1 medium carrot, grated
1 Tbsp flour
1 (450g) can creamed corn
2 cups boiling water
chopped parsley
fresh herbs
salt and pepper
sugar

In a large bowl or casserole dish, put butter, onion, celery and carrot. Cover and cook on High (100% power) for 8 minutes, stirring after 2 minutes. Stir in flour, then add creamed corn and boiling water. Cook, uncovered for 8-10 minutes longer, until bubbling, then taste and season as you like, adding fresh herbs, salt, pepper and a little sugar, if desired.

Brown Onion Soup

For 6 large servings:

2 Tbsp sugar
1 Tbsp water
75g butter
500g sliced onions
¼ cup flour
2½ Tbsp beef stock granules
5 cups boiling water
few drops hot pepper sauce
¼ cup dry sherry
12 diagonal slices French bread
butter for spreading
1 cup grated cheese
paprika

In a large high-heat resistant bowl, jug or casserole, heat sugar and water on High (100% power) for 2½-3 minutes or until dark brown. Watch closely, since cooking time varies. Do not let caramel blacken. Add butter and sliced onions. Cover and cook until onions are tender (8-10 minutes), stirring several times. Stir in flour and beef stock granules. Add 2 cups of the boiling water and a few drops of hot pepper sauce if desired. Cover and cook for 5 minutes longer. Add remaining 3 cups boiling water. Cook another 5 minutes. Add sherry. Butter the bread slices and microwave in one layer for 2 minutes. Sprinkle with grated cheese and paprika and heat until cheese melts. Reheat soup to boiling, stirring occcasionally. Pour each serving over one or two cheese croutons.

Alphabet Soup

For 2-3 servings:
2 tsp butter
1 small onion, chopped
1 stalk celery, sliced thin
1 small carrot, grated
¼ cup alphabet noodles
2 cups boiling water
2 tomatoes, chopped
1 tsp chicken stock granules
½ tsp sugar
fresh parsley or other fresh herbs

Put the first five ingredients into a bowl or large wide measuring jug. Add 1 cup boiling water. Cover tightly and cook on High (100% power) for 5 minutes, stirring after 3 minutes. Add remaining boiling water, chopped tomatoes, stock granules, sugar and herbs, and cook for 5 minutes longer.

Two Minute Noodle Soup

For 4 servings:
1 carrot
1 stalk celery
½ cup frozen peas
2 tsp butter
1 tsp light soya sauce
½ tsp sesame oil
*1 packet of 2-minute noodles
   (with stock sachet)*
3 cups boiling water
*½-1 cup shredded cooked chicken
   (optional)*
2 Tbsp dry sherry (optional)
2 spring onions

Cut the carrot and celery into strips the size of matches. Put into a bowl or casserole dish with the next four ingredients, the stock sachet, and the block of noodles, broken up. Pour 2 cups of the boiling water over all this. Cover and cook on High (100% power) for 5 minutes, stirring twice. Add the remaining boiling water, cooked chicken, the sherry, and the spring onions, sliced or cut into matchstick strips. Leave to stand for at least 5 minutes before serving, but preferably for longer. Reheat if necessary.

Special Chowder

This soup may be made with any combination of shellfish and fish.

For 4 large servings:
2 Tbsp butter
1 stalk celery, sliced

2 cloves garlic, chopped
2 Tbsp flour
1 cup dry white wine
1 (420g) can peeled tomatoes
   in juice
hot water
9-12 oysters
10-12 cooked mussels (optional)
100-200g scallops
400g fish fillets

In a large covered bowl or casserole dish heat the butter, celery and garlic on High (100% power) for 3 minutes, stirring after 1 minute. Add the flour and heat for 1 minute. Add the wine and heat 3 minutes longer. Stir until smooth and thick. Add the juice from the tomatoes and the oyster liquor, made up to 1½ cups with water. Heat until mixture is thick. If the scallops are large, cut them smaller. Cut the fish into pieces the same size as the scallops and oysters. Add all the seafood and fish to the soup. Heat 3 minutes or until fish is opaque.
Variations: Add fresh thyme, grated orange rind or saffron for extra flavour.

Shrimp Chowder

For 4 servings:
2 Tbsp butter
1 onion, chopped
2 cloves garlic, chopped
1 stalk celery, chopped
1 large potato, cubed (400g)
1 cup boiling water
1 tsp chicken stock granules
1 tsp green herbs stock granules
1 Tbsp cornflour
1½ cups milk
1 can shrimps (about 200g)
1 Tbsp chopped parsley

Heat butter, onion, garlic and celery in a covered bowl or casserole dish on High (100% power) for 3 minutes, shaking or stirring after 2 minutes. Add the scrubbed, cubed potato and the boiling water. Cover and cook for 6 minutes or until potato is tender. Stir in stock granules, the cornflour mixed to a paste with some of the milk, the remaining milk, shrimps and shrimp liquid. Heat chowder until it thickens, up to 8 minutes, stirring occasionally. Sprinkle with parsley. The shrimp flavour intensifies on standing.

Canned Asparagus Soup

The colour of this soup does not compare well with that of soup made with fresh asparagus, but you can make it at any time of the year with ingredients from your store cupboard.

For 4 servings:
2 Tbsp butter
1 onion, chopped
1 clove garlic, chopped
1 large potato, cubed
1 can (about 350g) asparagus
  spears
1 tsp chicken stock granules
1½ cups milk
salt and pepper

In bowl or casserole put the butter, onion and garlic. Cover and cook on High (100% power) for 5 minutes, stirring after 3 minutes. Add the potato and the liquid from the asparagus, made up to 1 cup with water. Cover and cook 5 minutes. Cut off and reserve heads from the asparagus spears. Purée cooked vegetables and the asparagus stalks. Sieve. Add stock granules and milk and reheat to boiling point, uncovered, stirring several times. Adjust seasoning to taste. Add reserved asparagus tips just before serving.

Fresh Tomato Soup

For 3-4 servings:
1 medium onion, very
  finely chopped
1 clove garlic, chopped
2 Tbsp butter
2 tsp cornflour
1 tsp salt
2 tsp sugar
¼ tsp paprika
500g ripe red tomatoes,
  skinned and chopped
½ cup hot water

In a large covered bowl or casserole dish cook the onion and garlic in the butter on High (100% power) for 4 minutes, stirring after 2 minutes. Stir in cornflour, then the remaining ingredients. Cook for 6-8 minutes until clear and slightly thickened.

Leek and Potato Soup

Although this soup is usually puréed, you can leave it chunky if you prefer a rough-textured soup.

For 4 servings:
2 large leeks (400g)
25g butter
2 medium potatoes, sliced
2 cups boiling water
2 tsp chicken stock granules
½ cup cream
½ cup milk

Slice leeks thinly, using only the white part. Place in large, covered bowl or casserole dish with the butter. Microwave on High (100% power) for 5 minutes. Add the scrubbed, peeled potatoes and 1 cup boiling water. Cover and cook for 5 minutes more, or until potato is tender. Purée if desired, and then add remaining boiling water and the chicken stock. Sieve mixture if desired. Add milk and cream. Reheat until boiling, stirring every 2-3 minutes. Season and serve.

Packet-Plus Soup

For 6 servings:
1 Tbsp butter
2 cloves garlic, crushed
1 onion, chopped
1 stalk celery, sliced
1 carrot, grated
½ cup chopped broccoli
½ cup sliced mushrooms
1 small can whole kernel corn
1 packet (3 serving size)
*   tomato soup*
½ cup cold water
2½ cups hot water

In a large covered bowl or casserole dish, heat the butter, garlic, onion, celery and carrot on High (100% power) for 5 minutes, stirring once. Add the broccoli, mushrooms and undrained corn. Cover and cook 4 minutes longer. In a cup mix the soup powder with the cold water. Stir into the cooked vegetables, with 2½ cups boiling water. Microwave, uncovered, for 8 minutes. Add fresh herbs, salt and pepper to taste.
Variations: Replace tomato soup with other (thick) packet soups. Vary the vegetables, depending on availability.

Oyster Soup

This is a very filling, creamy soup. Increase all quantities proportionately to suit your purpose. Larger quantities will require longer cooking times. Watch for the boiling point at each stage.

For 2 servings:
6 oysters and juice
2 Tbsp butter
1 clove garlic, chopped
¼ tsp grated nutmeg
freshly ground pepper
2 Tbsp flour
about 1¾ cups milk
1 Tbsp lemon juice

Drain oysters, reserving their liquid. Cut off the frilly beards from each oyster and put the beards in a bowl or casserole with the butter, garlic, nutmeg and pepper. Microwave on High (100% power) for about 2 minutes or until bubbling vigorously. Do not let butter brown. Stir in flour, then add the oyster liquor, made up to 2 cups with milk. Heat until thick and bubbling vigorously around the edge. Stir until smooth. Pour mixture through a sieve, pressing and then discarding the beards. Slice oyster bodies and add to soup. Add lemon juice, and salt to taste. Reheat when required, stirring several times. Overcooking toughens oysters.

Broccoli Cheese Soup

Overcooking spoils the colour of this soup. The puréed broccoli gives it an interesting, slightly grainy texture.

For 4-5 servings:
500g broccoli
2 Tbsp water
2 cloves garlic, chopped
25g butter
1 Tbsp flour
1 cup milk
1 tsp chicken stock granules
1 cup boiling water
1 cup grated cheese

Cut heads off broccoli. Peel stalks, discarding tough outer layer. Chop stalks finely and mix with heads in a large bowl or casserole dish. Add water, cover and cook on High (100% power) for 4 minutes or until tender but still bright green. Tip into food processor bowl. Heat garlic, butter, and flour for 1 minute, then stir in milk and stock granules. Heat until bubbling vigorously. Stir until smooth. Add boiling water and bring mixture back to boiling. Add cheese and stir until smooth. Purée broccoli, then add to soup. Reheat without boiling. Garnish with extra grated cheese if desired.
Variation: Add grated nutmeg to grated cheese.

Red Lentil Soup

Because lentils are the smallest members of the pulse family, they cook fastest, without soaking, to make a good substantial main course soup. Purée this or leave it plain.

For 4 servings:
½ cup red lentils
1 large carrot, grated
3 cloves garlic, chopped
2 Tbsp butter
½ tsp cumin seed (optional)
3½ cups boiling water
¼ tsp grated orange rind
(optional)
¾ tsp salt
½ tsp sugar (optional)
3-4 spring onions, chopped

Combine the first four ingredients in a large bowl or casserole. Add whole or ground cumin if you like its flavour, then pour in 2 cups of boiling water. Cover and microwave on High (100% power) for 15 minutes or until the lentils are tender. Add remaining water, and grated orange rind. Cook for 10 minutes longer. Add salt and a little sugar if desired. Purée if desired. Stir in spring onions. Taste and add a little more salt if necessary. (**Note:** Leave out the cumin and orange rind if you want a basic lentil soup.)

Green Pea and Potato Soup

You can alter the texture of this soup by puréeing it all, puréeing half of it, or leaving the whole lot chunky. It is good all ways!

For 4 servings:
1 rasher bacon, chopped
1 large onion, chopped
2 cloves garlic, chopped
1 Tbsp butter
2 medium potatoes, cubed
2 cups boiling water
1 tsp chicken stock granules
1 tsp sugar
2 mint sprigs
1 cup frozen peas
¼-½ cup cream

Combine first four ingredients in a covered bowl or high-sided casserole. Microwave on High (100% power) for 4 minutes. Add potatoes and 1 cup water. Cover and cook for 5 minutes. Add stock, sugar, mint and peas. Cook 2 minutes longer. Purée soup, adding remaining boiling water and the quantity of cream you like. Before serving, reheat until boiling, stirring several times.

Pea Soup with Bacon

Without prior soaking, the peas in this soup cook in 30 minutes. By thickening the cooked purée you get a smooth, creamy soup.

For 4 servings:
½ cup yellow split peas
1 large onion, chopped
2 slices bacon, chopped
3 cups boiling water
1 Tbsp butter
1 Tbsp flour
¼ cup cold water
salt and pepper

Combine first three ingredients with 2 cups boiling water in a covered bowl or high sided casserole.
Microwave on Medium (50% power) for 30 minutes. Purée preferably in food processor. Melt butter on High (100% power) for 30 seconds. Stir in flour and heat 30 seconds more. Stir in the cold water, then the boiling water. Cook until this thickens and boils vigorously. Stir well and add to puréed peas (in food processor). Mix well. Reheat until soup bubbles vigorously. Taste and adjust seasonings, if necessary. Serve immediately and reheat when required. Garnish with sliced frankfurter or cooked sausage when serving, if desired.

Pumpkin Soup

This soup will brighten the coldest winter night. Use any member of the pumpkin family to make it.

For 6-8 servings:
1kg pumpkin
1 large onion, quartered
2 cloves garlic, chopped
¼ cup cold water
1½ tsp chicken stock granules
1½ tsp green herb stock granules
1½ tsp sugar
½ tsp nutmeg
3 cups boiling water
¼ cup cream (optional)

Cut pumpkin into several, fairly evenly shaped pieces. Remove seeds but not the skin if it is tough, since it is easy to lift flesh away from skin when cooked. Place the pumpkin, the quartered onion and the garlic with the cold water in a large covered container. Microwave on High (100% power) for 10 minutes, or until tender. (Smaller pieces cook faster.) Do not overcook. When cool enough to work with, scrape pumpkin from the skin and purée the flesh, with the cooked onion, garlic and liquid, using a food processor, if available. Add stock granules, sugar, nutmeg and 1 cup boiling water to make a thick purée. Sieve to remove any lumps. Return mixture to casserole or soup tureen. Add the remaining boiling water. Stir to mix. Reheat until very hot, stirring every two minutes. Add cream before serving, if desired.

Spinach Soup

The colour and flavour of this soup depends upon cooking the spinach just the right amount.

For 4-5 servings:
250g spinach
2 Tbsp butter
1 onion, chopped
1 clove garlic, chopped
1 tsp chicken stock granules
¼ tsp grated nutmeg
2 Tbsp flour
1½ cups milk
½ cup boiling water
salt and pepper

Wash spinach carefully. Pull off and discard stems. Cook, without any added water, in an oven bag loosely fastened with a rubber band, or in a covered bowl or casserole dish, on High (100% power) for 2-3 minutes or until leaves are wilted and tender but still brightly coloured. Purée, preferably in a food processor or blender. In covered bowl or casserole dish cook butter, onion and garlic for 3 minutes, stirring after 1 minute. Stir in flavourings and flour and microwave 30 seconds. Add milk. Microwave for about 3 minutes more, stirring every minute. When sauce bubbles vigorously around the edge, stir well, then cook until edge bubbles again, about 1 minute. Add boiling water to puréed spinach, then add this to the sauce, stirring well. Taste and add a little salt and pepper to balance flavour, if necessary. Reheat until very hot, but not boiling.

Curried Kumara Soup

Unbelievably smooth and creamy, this soup may be thinned to the desired consistency.

For 4-6 servings:
500g kumara
50g butter
2 cloves garlic, chopped
½ tsp curry powder
1 cup boiling water
2 tsp chicken stock granules
2-3 cups milk

Peel kumara, using a potato peeler. Slice thinly. Microwave butter, garlic and curry powder in a large bowl or casserole dish on High (100% power) for 1½ minutes or until bubbling. Add sliced kumara and boiling water. Cover. Cook until kumara is tender, about 10 minutes. Add stock granules. Purée, thinning with 2 cups milk. Return mixture to casserole dish. Add extra milk, if desired. Reheat, stirring every 2 minutes, until mixture bubbles around edges and soup has heated evenly. Taste and adjust seasonings.

Fish

Fish

Fish microwaves wonderfully well! Its flavour and texture is excellent and it cooks in next to no time.

RULES FOR MICROWAVING FISH

- Use high (100%) power
- Allow about 1 minute per 100g fish, a little more for thicker pieces and less for thinner ones.
- Cook fish until it whitens and turns opaque. Test it to see if it flakes slightly after leaving it to stand for 30-60 seconds per 100g, after cooking.
- Always allow standing time after microwaving fish.
- Nearly always cover fish with cling wrap during cooking so it cooks more evenly. Remove it after the standing time.
- Put thicker pieces towards the edge of the dish.
- Turn fillets in melted butter or brush with melted plain or garlic butter before cooking.
- Where whole fish is thickest, cut it to the bone in several places for even cooking.
- If you want to cook fish without a recipe, sprinkle the buttered surface with paprika, garlic salt and any chopped fresh herbs you like.
- If you want crunchy fish, sprinkle cooked fish with crisp crumbs before serving it.
- Overcooking dries out, shrinks and toughens fish. Take great care not to spoil fish by overcooking it.

You may well find that you make only "Easy Fish Fillets" because this recipe is so easy, fast and good, that you can enjoy it time and time again. You can use your microwave to cook one fish for yourself (in one or two minutes) or present a wonderfully elaborate fish meal for your next lunch or dinner party.

Unless you have a browning dish you will not be able to microwave "Fried" Fish, but I think that after you have tried the other fish recipes, you may feel that you can live without fried fish!

There are several points and techniques which will help you microwave fish to perfection relatively inexpensively.

Start with fresh or good quality frozen fish. (This applies to all fish cooking, of course.)

Don't have fixed or set ideas about the particular type of fish you want to use for a particular recipe. In the recipes that follow you can use many different fish. Look at the photos for the shapes and sizes of fish used.

The most widely known and used fish are likely to be the most expensive and they may not always be available. See if you can find another fish of the same texture and thickness, and try it instead. It will usually taste just as good.

Flatfish have a distinctive shape. Their fillets are thin and roll or fold easily. If they are not available, cut other fine textured fish in thinner slices and use them instead. You will find it easier to cut frozen fish while it is still partly frozen. You can cook it from this stage, too. Cook one fillet or small whole fish on the plate on which you will serve it.

Don't be frightened of cooking whole fish. They are very easy to work with in the microwave oven. I have even microwaved "just caught" fish without scaling or gutting them.

Immediately after cooking I peel off the skin and scales together and lift the cooked boneless fillets away from the carcase, discarding everything else. (This is a wonderful technique to deal with small fish caught from a jetty!)

If you don't have a suitable cooking dish, use a large oven bag. Lay the fish on it on a concave surface. Add cooking liquid, etc., gather up the bag at each end of the fish and secure with a rubber band. If the bag won't meet over the top of the fish, top it with a piece of cling wrap.

Because fish cooks so fast, you can cook one serving after another on individual plates, if you like.

I don't leave vents when I cover fish with cling wrap. This means that it puffs up a little as the fish cooks, and as soon as it is finished, during the standing stime, it sucks down, clinging to the fish and plate. I think the fish is improved and compacted by this method. Try it and see!

Shellfish may be opened and cooked very easily in the microwave. For best flavour and results, put them in a covered container with a little, well-flavoured liquid.

Microwave them until the muscle that attaches them to the shell separates from it.
(1 kg mussels open in 6-8 minutes.)
Overcooking shrinks and toughens shellfish. The liquid from steamed shellfish makes wonderful fish-cooking liquid if saved.
Fish flavourings and garnishes include: thyme, marjoram, chervil, spring onions, chillis, root ginger, paprika, dill, bayleaves, lemons, fennel, celery, coriander leaf (Chinese parsley), tarragon, chives, peppercorns, cress, garlic, cucumber and parsley.

Sauteed Fish Steaks

You need a browning dish for this recipe.

For 1 serving:
1 fish steak, about 1cm thick (250g)
flour for coating
1 tsp butter or oil

Preheat microwave browning dish on High (100% power) for 6 minutes.
Lightly flour the fish steak. To the browning dish add the butter or oil, then the fish. Microwave for 1 minute. Turn and microwave about 1½ minutes more, or until cooked as desired.

Small Whole Flatfish

For minimum dishwashing, cook these one at a time, on individual serving plates.

For 1 serving:
1 sole or flounder (about 200g)
2 tsp butter
1 clove garlic, chopped
paprika

For even cooking, cut the cleaned, scalded fish several times on each side, to the backbone. Heat butter and garlic on High (100% power) until bubbling (about 1 minute). Brush garlic butter over lower, then upper surface of fish, especially into cuts. Sprinkle with paprika. Place fish on a serving plate, cover whole plate with cling wrap and cook for 2 minutes. Stand 2 minutes before removing wrap to serve.

"Fried" Fish Fillets

For crisply coated microwaved fish, use a browning dish.

2 100g fish fillets
2 Tbsp flour
¼ tsp each paprika, curry powder, celery salt and onion salt
milk for dipping
2 Tbsp cooking oil

Combine flour, paprika, curry powder, celery salt and onion salt. Dip fillets first in milk, then in this coating. Stand on rack while preheating browning dish, on High (100% power) for 6 minutes. Quickly put oil in hot browning dish and microwave fillets for 1½ minutes. Turn and cook about 1½ minutes longer, until flesh flakes.

Stuffed Flatfish

Smooth textured stuffing "dresses up" this fish, making it much more substantial.

For 2 servings:
1 sole or flounder (200g)
75g boneless fish fillets
25g smoked salmon or shrimp
2 Tbsp cream
1 tsp tomato concentrate
½ tsp salt
1 Tbsp melted butter

Cut fish down its midline between head and tail. Run knife along backbone, lifting fillets on each side. If you want a boneless stuffed fish, cut under the backbone and remove it. Otherwise, pack stuffing on top of backbone.
For Stuffing: Mix next 5 ingredients in food processor until well blended. Pack stuffing into cavity of fish. Brush skin with melted butter. Cover with cling-wrap. Microwave on High (100% power) for 3 minutes. Let stand for 2 minutes. Uncover. Garnish with sour cream, lump fish roe, etc.
or lie a row of lemon slices over stuffing, before serving.
Variation: For economy, replace salmon or shrimp with extra fish fillet. Appearance will still be good.

Simmered Seafood

To make this delicious fish mixture, microwave all the different ingredients separately so that nothing overcooks. Decide which shellfish you will remove from their shells, strain and then thicken the accumulated cooking liquid, cook the cubed fish, and reheat everything together.

When you buy the shellfish, allow one or two items per serving, rather than buying by weight. Use whatever shellfish is available. If the worst comes to the worst, use only fish, but don't expect the flavour to be the same!

For 4 servings:
½ cup white wine
2 garlic cloves
1 bayleaf
6 peppercorns
herbs or saffron (optional)
8 mussels (400g)
8 cockles (200g)
8 pipis or tuatuas (200g)
8 scallops (100-150g)
4 green prawns (100g)
500g fish fillets
2 Tbsp water and white wine
2 Tbsp butter
2 Tbsp flour

Put wine, crushed garlic, bayleaf, peppercorns (and other herbs or a pinch of saffron threads) in a fairly large microwave casserole with a lid. Add the mussels, microwave on High (100% power) about 2 minutes, or until shells open. Lift the mussels onto a tray. In same liquid, microwave cockles, then pipis, until they open (1-2 minutes). Pierce scallop roes. Microwave scallops in liquid 2-3 minutes, until opaque. Remove. Microwave prawns until pink (1½-2 minutes).

Strain liquid into a measuring jug and make up to 1½ cups with water or a water-wine mixture. Melt butter, add flour and microwave 30 seconds. Add strained liquid and heat to boiling, about 2 minutes. Whisk until smooth. Taste, adjust seasonings, and add 2-3 Tbs cream if desired. (This makes the sauce rich but the flavour bland). Add fish cut into 2cm cubes. Microwave about 4 minutes, until opaque. Add cooked shellfish, in or out of their shells, according to your preference. Reheat when required.

Variations: (a) After cooking fish fillets, divide everything between individual serving plates. Reheat plates separately when required. (b) Serve with a spoon and fork, crusty bread, and a side salad. (c) Use whatever combination of seafood appeals to you!

Oyster-Stuffed Fillets

You need only a few oysters to flavour these quickly-prepared but elegant stuffed fillets.

For 4-6 servings:
500-600g boneless fish fillets
50g butter
¼ cup finely chopped onion
1 cup soft breadcrumbs
½ dozen oysters, thinly sliced
¼ cup finely chopped onion
1 cup soft breadcrumbs
½ dozen oysters, thinly sliced
¼ cup finely chopped parsley
1 Tbsp parmessan cheese
½ tsp paprika
½ tsp garlic salt

Select small flatfish fillets or cut thicker roundfish fillets diagonally into thinner fillet-shaped slices, making 8-12 pieces altogether. In dish big enough to hold folded fillets in one layer, melt butter. Tip half of the melted butter into another bowl, add the onion, cover and microwave on High (100% power) for 2 minutes. Stir in the breadcrumbs, the oysters and half of the parsley. Lay fish pieces in a row on the bench skin side up. Place equal amounts of stuffing on one end of each. Fold other end over stuffing.

Place stuffed fish into the buttered dish, with rounded sides to edge of dish. Stir together the cheese, paprika, garlic salt and remaining parsley. Sprinkle over fillets. Cover with cling wrap and microwave for 3-4 minutes, or until opaque. Stand 2-3 minutes before uncovering.

Orange Fish Steaks

For this recipe, the sauce is cooked before the fish.

For 2 servings:
2 fish steaks, 200g each
1 Tbsp butter
1 tsp cornflour
juice and grated rind of 1 orange

Melt butter in microwave on High (100% power) for about ½ minute. Add cornflour, orange juice and grated orange rind. Microwave until sauce bubbles and thickens. Place the steaks on a plate with the thinner sections near the centre. Spread the sauce over the fish. Cover with cling wrap. Microwave for 3½ minutes. Allow to stand for 3 minutes before uncovering and serving.

Easy Fish Fillets

Try this very simple, but very good recipe before you experiment with other more complicated mixtures.

For 4 servings:
4 fish fillets (100-150g each)
1½ Tbsp butter
1 tsp garlic salt
½ tsp paprika
2 Tbsp chopped parsley (or other fresh herb)

Melt butter on High (100% power) in a dish large enough to hold fillets in one layer (about 1 minute). Turn fillets in the melted butter. Arrange fish in the dish with thicker parts towards the edges. Sprinkle with garlic salt, paprika and parsley, using more or less seasoning, according to taste. Cover with cling wrap and microwave for 4-5 minutes, until the fish is opaque in the thickest parts. Let stand for 2-3 minutes before uncovering.

Creamy Paprika Fish

Quick, easy, and very good!

For 3-4 servings
1 large onion, chopped
1 Tbsp butter
500g boneless fish fillets, cubed
½ tsp celery salt
2 tsp cornflour
½ cup evaporated milk
½ tsp paprika
2 spring onions, chopped

Put chopped onion and butter into a 20-22cm microwave cooking/serving dish. Cover and microwave on High (100% power) for 3 minutes, stirring once. Add fish cut into 15mm cubes. Sprinkle with celery salt and cornflour and turn to mix. Add evaporated milk and mix again.
Sprinkle with paprika and spring onions, cover and cook for 3 minutes. Stand 1 minute before uncovering.
Fish is cooked when the centre is opaque. Cook 1 minute longer if necessary. Before serving sprinkle with extra paprika if desired.
Varation: Sprinkle with grated cheese before adding extra paprika.
After cooking: Microwave until cheese melts.

Salmon-stuffed Rolls

For 4 servings:
*4 large or 8 small flatfish
   fillets (about 400g)
50g thinly sliced salmon
¼-½ cup sour cream
2 Tbsp chopped chives or spring
   onion leaves
2 Tbsp white wine
2 Tbsp cream or crème frâiche
1 tsp mixed mustard*

Lay fillets skin-side up. Spread with
(a) salmon (b) then sour cream (c)
then chives or spring onions.
Roll up, thin end first. After rolling
up, cut large rolls made from large
fillets into two shorter rolls. Secure
each roll with a toothpick. Arrange
rolls like pinwheels in dish large
enough to hold them in one layer
without crowding. Add wine, cover
and microwave on High (100%
power) for 5 minutes, or until fish
is opaque at the thickest part.
Lift fish from dish and remove
toothpicks. Add cream and mixed
mustard to remaining liquid.
Microwave for 3 minutes or until
thick. Replace fillets in sauce and
heat if necessary before serving.
Variation: Replace salmon with
pureed fish, as in Stuffed Flatfish.

Fish Ragout

Use medium to firm textured fish.

For 4-6 servings:
*50g butter
2 onions, sliced
2 garlic cloves, chopped
¼ cup water
½ cup white wine
1 cup peeled cubed tomatoes
1 tsp salt
½ tsp sugar
1 tsp fresh thyme leaves
¼ cup chopped parsley
600g boneless fish pieces
2-3 tsp cornflour*

Microwave butter, onions and garlic
in a large, covered dish on High
(100% power) for 5-6 minutes,
stirring after 1½ minutes. Add
water, wine, tomatoes, seasonings
and herbs. (Replace wine with ½
cup water and 2 Tbsp lemon juice if
desired). Cut fish into fingers 8 x
2cm wide and add to the mixture,
with cornflour. Mix well. Cover and
microwave 4-6 minutes until fish is
firm, opaque and flakes easily.

Sesame Squid

Cooked briefly, squid is very
tender. Its delicate flavour blends
well with this sauce.

For 1-2 servings:
*200g squid
1 tsp grated root ginger
2 cloves garlic
2 tsp sesame oil
1 Tbsp corn or soya oil
100g mushrooms, sliced
½ cup chopped spring onions
½ tsp instant chicken stock
2 tsp cornflour
2 tsp light soya sauce
1 Tbsp dry sherry
2 Tbsp water*

Heat a browning dish on High
(100% power) for 6 minutes. Cut
squid into 1cm. squares. Mix with
grated ginger, crushed garlic, and
the two oils. Put aside. Combine
chopped mushrooms and spring
onions. Mix remaining ingredients
to a smooth paste. Add squid to hot
browning dish. Stir for 30 seconds.
Add mushroom mixture. Cover and
microwave for 1 minute. Stir in
paste. Cover again and cook 2
minutes longer, until thickened.
Serve on rice.

Layered Fish Mousse

Using a food processor and a microwave oven, you can make this spectacular fish mousse in less than half an hour. What's more, you can make it ahead and reheat it! Serve it plain or with crème frâiche flavoured with tomato concentrate and thinned with white wine and lemon juice to suit your own taste.

For 8-10 small servings:
(for the white layers)
1½ *cups fresh breadcrumbs*
6 *spring onions, chopped finely*
750g *cubed boneless snapper,*
    blue cod, tarakihi or
    orange roughy
2 *small eggs*
3 Tbsp *lemon juice*
2 tsp *salt*
½ *cup cream*
½ *cup milk*
(for coloured layers)
100g *smoked salmon, drained*
canned salmon, or drained shrimps
1 Tbsp *tomato concentrate*
½ *cup frozen peas*
2 Tbsp *chopped parsley*
1 Tbsp *chopped fresh dill*
    (optional)

Divide the first 8 ingredients into two equal parts. (The food processor cannot mix more than half at a time.) Each part will be handled in a different way. In a food processor purée white part of spring onions, fish, eggs, lemon juice and salt until smooth. Add breadcrumbs, then cream and milk gradually, processing until fluffy.
Part 1: (3 white layers) Divide the mixture into 3 equal quantities. Spread ⅓ in a microwave loaf pan, about 20 x 10 x 8cm, which has been lined with baking paper or cling wrap.
Save the other ⅔ mixture for the middle and top layers.
Part 2: (1 green layer and 1 orange layer). Remove half of this mixture (which will later be coloured green), leave half in the food processor. To the food processor add the salmon (or shrimps) and tomato concentrate. Process to a smooth puree. Spread over the first white layer in loaf pan.
Cover the orange-coloured layer with the second of the white layers. If difficult to spread evenly, divide it into blobs first, then spread with a wet rubber spatula.
Process unthawed frozen peas with ½ cup chopped green spring onion leaves, parsley and dill leaf if available. When finely chopped, add remaining half of second fish mixture and combine well. Spread over second layer. Cover green layer with remaining white fish. Wrap baking paper or cling wrap over last layer. Microwave on 60% power for 12-15 minutes or until centre springs back and small knife cuts clean in centre. Leave to stand at least 10 minutes. Unmould. Serve hot or cold.

Whole Fish with Lemon Sauce

It is much easier to lift pieces of cooked fish off the bone than to bone the fish before cooking. If you prefer to dismember your cooked fish in private, cool fish after microwaving and remove skin and bones. Pour sauce over fish, then reheat, adding garnishes just before serving.

For 4 servings:
1 whole round fish (750g)
fresh herbs
1 clove garlic (optional)
1 lemon, halved lengthwise,
    then sliced
2 Tbsp melted butter
1 egg yolk
1 Tbsp lemon juice
½ tsp cornflour
¼ tsp garlic salt

Place fish on serving platter. (If necessary, remove head and tail so fish fits both the platter and the oven.) Cut several parallel slashes on fish so that the thicker part will cook more evenly and quickly. For extra flavour, insert fresh herbs, garlic and lemon slices in the body cavity and in the cuts. Brush both sides of fish with plain or garlic-flavoured melted butter. Cover with cling wrap. Microwave on High (100% power) for 6-7 minutes. Stand for 2 minutes and then remove wrap, checking to see if flesh at thickest part is opaque and will flake. Pour liquid from the fish into a bowl containing the egg yolk, lemon juice, cornflour and garlic salt. Whisk to mix. Microwave sauce 1½ minutes, or until it thickens. Do not overheat. Pour sauce over the fish.
Variation: For a more colourful surface, use the same coating as in Oyster-Stuffed Fillets, sprinkling on the coating before cooking.

Sesame-Steamed Fish

You can make this interesting, well flavoured fish with very little time and trouble in a microwave oven. Select a microwave-proof platter large enough to hold the fish with its head and tail intact. If the tail extends over the edge of the dish and will not fit in the oven, cut it off, heat it separately on High (100% power) for 30 seconds, and put it in place again for presentation.

For 4 servings:
1 whole fish (600-750g)
3-4 spring onions
2cm length root ginger
2 Tbsp soya sauce
1 Tbsp sesame oil

Slash thickest part of fish with several parallel cuts on each side. Cut spring onions into 2cm lengths. Peel root ginger. Slice onions and ginger into matchstick strips. Sprinkle half of these on the plate, lay the fish on them, and then sprinkle the rest over it. Sprinkle the soya sauce and sesame oil evenly over the fish. Mask head or eye section with aluminium foil if desired, making sure it will not touch the sides of the oven. Cover with cling wrap. Microwave on High (100% power), allowing 50 seconds per 100g of fish. Stand, covered, for 4 minutes. Uncover and check to see if flesh at thickest part is opaque and will flake. If not, microwave 1-2 minutes longer. Baste with juices. Serve with unthickened juice, and with parsley or Chinese parsley garnish. To serve, lift fish from bone, starting from back.
Variations: (a) Just before serving, heat 1 Tbsp sesame oil until very hot. Drizzle over the cooked fish, which will sizzle. (b) Use the same ingredients, replacing whole fish with boned, skinned fillets. Grate ginger and chop spring onions more finely, if desired. Allow same cooking time per 100g.

Herbed Whole Fish

For this easily-prepared dish use any small whole sea or freshwater fish.

For 2 servings:
2 small salmon, trout or other small
*   fish (100-150g each)*
fresh herbs
lemon slices
2 shallots
2 Tbsp butter
2 cloves garlic
Topping for Fish:
2 Tbsp butter
¼ cup slivered almonds

With small pieces of foil, mask the head and tail to prevent overcooking. (**Note:** *The foil must not touch the side of the oven.*) Fill the fish cavity with fresh herbs, slices of lemon and chopped shallots. Heat the butter and garlic on High (100% power) for 1½ minutes or until bubbling. Brush over fish. On a flat plate, arrange the fish with the thicker part towards the outside of the dish. Cover the fish and plate with cling wrap. Microwave for 4 minutes. In a small bowl microwave the butter and almonds for 2 minutes or until lightly brown. Spoon onto the fish before serving.

Fish in Parsley Sauce

There are times when plain, old-fashioned food is all you want. Serve this on buttered toast, rice or noodles.

For 4 servings:
2 Tbsp butter
2 Tbsp flour
2 Tbsp chopped parsley
1 cup milk
½ tsp celery, onion, or
*   garlic salt*
400-500g fish fillets

Melt butter on High (100% power) for 30 seconds. Stir in flour and microwave 30 seconds. Add parsley, milk and seasoned salt. Cook until boiling, about 2 minutes, then beat until smooth. While sauce cooks, cut fish into 2cm cubes or larger pieces. Stir fish into thick sauce. Cover and microwave 4-5 minutes or until fish is opaque. Serve immediately or reheat when required.

Quick Kedgeree

You do not need to pre-cook the smoked fish for this recipe.

For 3-4 servings:
2 eggs
400-500g smoked fish
2 Tbsp butter
4 spring onions, chopped
2 cups cooked rice

Add eggs to small, flat bottomed dish containing ¼ cup boiling water. Cover. Microwave on High (100% power) until yolks harden (about 2½ minutes). Skin and bone fish and cut flesh into small pieces. In dish large enough to cook and serve the kedgeree, melt butter for 1 minute. Toss fish in butter. Add spring onions and cooked (preferably unsalted) rice. Drain eggs, chop and stir into fish mixture. Cover and microwave 4-6 minutes, stirring after 3 minutes. Taste and add more seasonings if necessary. Note: If using hot smoked fish, flake instead of cutting, if desired.

Quick Shrimp Creole

Prepare this ahead, then leave to stand to blend flavours.

For 4 servings:
250g shelled shrimp, fresh or frozen
2 Tbsp butter
2 cloves garlic
2 Tbsp flour
10-12 drops hot pepper sauce
1 Tbsp tomato concentrate
1 green pepper, chopped
1 (420g) can whole tomatoes
in juice, chopped

Thaw shrimp if necessary. In a flat-bottomed microwave dish, melt butter on High (100% power) for 30 seconds. Stir in chopped garlic and flour. Microwave 2 minutes, until light brown. Add the remaining ingredients. Heat until bubbling and thickened, 4-5 minutes. Add shrimp (and liquid) and reheat until sauce bubbles again. Taste and adjust seasonings, adding salt, sugar and basil, if desired.

Crayfish Mornay

Prepare this ahead and reheat individual servings when required.

For 2 servings:
1 cooked crayfish (400g)
1 Tbsp butter
1 Tbsp flour
¼ cup milk
¼ cup wine or milk
1 cup grated tasty cheese
3-4 drops hot pepper sauce
1 tsp chopped chives
2 tsp chopped spring onion
pinch of paprika

Halve the crayfish and cube the flesh (175-200g). Remove the legs and save for garnish. Microwave the butter and flour on High (100% power) for 1 minute. Stir in the first measure of milk. Microwave 1 minute. Add remaining liquid and microwave until sauce thickens. Stir in the hot sauce and ¾ of the cheese, saving the remainder for topping. Reheat sauce to melt cheese. Add the crayfish to the sauce and spoon the mixture into both shells. Place each on a serving plate. Sprinkle with the remaining cheese, chives, spring onions, and paprika. Reheat each plate for 1½ minutes, until flesh is hot and cheese is partially melted. Arrange the legs attractively and serve.

Garlic Mussels

Cook these in individual serving bowls.

For each serving:
mussels (300g or about 6)
1 clove garlic
2 tsp butter
1-2 bayleaves
¼ cup white wine
2 Tbsp chopped parsley

Scrub the mussels and put aside. Chop the garlic, add butter and microwave on High (100% power) for 1 minute on the serving bowl. Add bay leaves, wine and chopped parsley. Place the mussels in bowl, hinged end down. Cover with cling wrap. Microwave for 2 minutes or until shells have opened and mussels have separated from the shells. Do not overcook. Lift off wrap, pull off the beards and serve immediately with French bread to soak up cooking liquid.

Buttered Mussels

Prepare these delicious mussels on their half shells for a few individual servings, or serve them out of their shells for an easy appetiser for larger groups.

For 4-6 servings
24-36 cooked mussels
50g butter
2-4 garlic cloves, chopped
2 Tbsp lemon juice
4 drops hot pepper sauce
¼ cup chopped parsley (or
   mixed fresh herbs)

Buy steamed mussels or precook them yourself and arrange them in their half shells. In a loosely covered bowl microwave the butter, garlic, lemon juice and pepper sauce until hot and bubbling, on High (100% power) for about 2½ minutes. Then:
(a) Mix all the mussels in butter to coat evenly and microwave for about 2 minutes, until mussels are warm and plumped, or
(b) Brush hot butter over mussels on the half shell. Arrange about 6 shells on each plate. Cover with cling wrap. When required, heat each plate for about 30 seconds or until you hear the first spatter.
Note: Do not overcook or mussels will shrink and toughen.

Meat & Poultry

Meat and Poultry

Meat cooking patterns vary from family to family, depending on the meat used, the style of cooking preferred, and past successes and failures in the preparation of family meals. Many meats microwave very well, saving time and effort. The meat and poultry section of this book contains recipes which I consider microwave well.

The times given are for meat cooked from room temperature. Meat refrigerated will require longer cooking.

Always thaw meat at low power levels before cooking it at higher power levels.

Different power levels are required for different meats. In general, only very tender meat from a young animal or bird is cooked at high power levels.

Exceptions to this are mince and sausagemeat, which microwave very well at high power levels. Take care not to overcook microwaved meat or it will be tough and dry. Always allow for more cooking during the standing time. Don't worry about lack of colour in microwaved meat. Longer-cooking meats brown naturally, and it is easy to improve the colour of short-cooking meats with marinades and seasonings. Watch for end points rather than following the given times exactly, since these can vary quite a lot. Use the following recipes just as they are, or use them as guides when you want to microwave your favourite meat recipes.

BEEF

Corned beef silverside microwaves very well at a low power level. It reheats well, too.

Small roasts from the loin area and rump cook very well. They are better served rare or medium rather than well done.

Do not microwave rolled roasts from the shoulder.

One or two tender steaks cook well in a browning dish, but larger numbers are better cooked in a frying pan.

Thinly sliced beef cooks very quickly, in many different recipes, but toughens if overcooked. "Stir-fried" marinated beef is particularly successful, when microwaved.

Microwaved beef stews and casseroles need low power levels. Minced beef is excellent when microwaved.

LAMB

Because lamb is tender, young meat, it microwaves well. Fat should be trimmed off, whenever possible. Bone-in legs often need the shank end shielded with foil to prevent over-cooking. Boneless legs, being a more even shape, cook more evenly, uncovered or in oven bags.

Since the meat from the loin is especially tender, it microwaves particularly well.

A well trimmed rack is tender enough to cook at High power level.

PORK

Shoulder roasts of pork cook very well. I always check the internal temperatures of these fairly large roasts with a meat thermometer. I prefer to cook pork chops conventionally but pork fillets microwave very well indeed. Thinly sliced pork "stir fries" well, and pork schnitzels, banged thinner after cutting fairly thin, cook quickly. Take care not to let them overcook and dry out. Minced pork cooks very successfully, and microwaved bacon is very popular and quick. Pork spareribs microwave well at low power levels.

I prefer to microwave thinly sliced pork rather than cubed pork in sauced mixtures.

Sausagemeat microwaves very well, but does not have a crisp crust unless cooked in a browning dish.

CHICKEN

Chicken microwaves particularly well. Microwaved chicken thighs and drumsticks are especially good. Use coatings and marinades for colour and texture when microwaving this quickly cooked meat. (A drumstick cooks in 2 minutes, and a thigh in 2-3 minutes.) I think chicken breasts are better when microwaved than cooked conventionally.

Pre-cooked (barbecued, rotisseried and smoked) whole chickens or chicken meat may be reheated in the microwave oven.

Whole chickens microwave very well, but look best and cook more evenly if "bagged" first. Use marinades and coatings for extra colour.

Any skinless boned chicken meat may be sliced for microwaved "stir-fried" chicken recipes. Take care not to overcook it.

I microwave "grand poulets" very successfully, but usually cook larger turkeys conventionally.

Corned Beef

Save time, stop cooking smells and steam.

1-1½kg corned silverside
bay leaf, garlic clove, parsley, or
celery, mustard seeds, peppercorns,
orange rind, coriander seeds etc.
2 cups boiling water

Soak the meat for 1-2 hours in cold water if you think it may be salty. Place the drained beef in casserole with whatever selection of seasonings you like. Pour water over the meat.

Cook on (30% power) for 30 minutes per 500g. Turn twice during cooking. Leave to stand in cooking liquid for 30 minutes before serving hot with mustard sauce. If serving cold, refrigerate in bag with about ½ cup cooking liquid.

Mustard Sauce
2 Tbsp butter
2 Tbsp flour
1 Tbsp mixed mustard
1 cup beef cooking liquid or ½ cup
*   beef liquid and ½ cup water*
2 tsp wine vinegar (optional) or
2-3 Tbsp cream or crème fraîche
(optional)

Heat butter and flour on High (100% power) for 1 minute. Stir in the mixed mustard, then ½ cup beef cooking liquid. Heat until mixture bubbles and thickens. Stir and taste. Add another ½ cup more cooking liquid, or water if sauce is too salty. Add wine vinegar if you like a tangy sauce, cream or crème fraîche if you want to soften the flavours.

Stir-fried Beef

For this recipe use very thin slices of beef, cut across the grain of the meat, from flank skirt or blade steak or cut beef schnitzels in strips about 1cm x 5cm. Trim away all fat and connective tissue.

For 4 servings:
500g thinly sliced beef
2 cloves garlic, chopped
4 Tbsp oil
1 Tbsp sherry
1 Tbsp dark soya sauce
2 tsp cornflour
2 tsp brown sugar
1 tsp beef stock granules
400g sliced vegetables

Put sliced meat in an oven bag with half the oil and all remaining ingredients except the vegetables. Knead bag thoroughly to mix. Leave to stand for at least 15 minutes. Secure with rubber band, leaving a finger-sized hole. Put bag so meat mixture is spread evenly, fairly flat. Select quick-cooking, tender vegetables, e.g. mushrooms, snowpeas, broccoli, cauli, celery, spring onions, young cabbage, bean sprouts, spinach. Slice into thin slices. Coat with remaining oil. In a covered microwave casserole cook on High (100% power) for 3-4 minutes, until just tender. Microwave meat in oven bag for 3-4 minutes until no longer pink. Add to vegetables stirring to coat. Serve immediately. If vegetables have made liquid, add a little extra cornflour paste and microwave 30 seconds to thicken. Serve on rice or noodles.

Beef Stroganoff

For 2-3 servings:
250g rump steak, sliced 5mm thick
50g butter
2 onions, sliced
1 cup (100g) sliced mushrooms
1 Tbsp flour
½ tsp paprika
½ cup white wine
2 tsp tomato concentrate
¼ cup sour cream or crème fraîche
¾ tsp salt
¼ cup chopped parsley

Slice rump steak into 5mm ribbons, melt butter in large microwave dish. Add onions, mix, cover and cook on High (100% power) for 4 minutes. Add mushrooms, the flour-coated meat and paprika. Stir, cover, and cook 2-3 minutes until meat loses its pinkness. Stir in wine and tomato concentrate, heat 1 minute or until liquid thickens. Stir in sour cream, salt and half the parsley. Reheat but do not boil. Sprinkle with remaining parsley. Serve with noodles.

Barbecued Beef

For 2 servings:
2 hamburger buns or lengths of
  French bread
1 mild onion, very finely chopped
1 Tbsp oil
2 Tbsp tomato ketchup
2 tsp tomato concentrate
1 Tbsp brown sugar
2 tsp worcestershire sauce
1 tsp mixed mustard
200g thinly sliced raw or cooked
  beef

Split bread and toast, if desired. Mix onion and oil in covered microwave dish. Cook on High (100% power) for 3 minutes. Add next 5 ingredients. Heat 3 minutes or until sauce bubbles. Stir in beef, coating well with sauce. Cover. If using raw beef, microwave for 3-4 minutes, until beef loses its pink colour. Heat cooked beef for 1-2 minutes or until hot. Spoon meat and sauce into buns. Reheat if desired. Serve with salad.

Beef (or Pork) Olives

These cook in an unbelievably short time. Overcooking toughens them so take care!

For 4 servings:
400g thinly sliced beef or pork schnitzels

Stuffing:
½ cup cooked rice
½ cup chopped pineapple
3 spring onions
2 Tbsp beaten raw egg
¼ tsp curry powder

Coating:
1 Tbsp sherry
1 Tbsp dark soya sauce
1 Tbsp tomato concentrate
2 tsp cornflour

Trim connective tissue and fat from schnitzels. Cut into 8 pieces. If pieces aren't thin enough, place between sheets of plastic and pound with a rolling pin. Mix Stuffing ingredients. Divide among 8 schnitzels. Roll each up, making parcels filled with stuffing. Arrange evenly around the edge of a circular dish (or in a ring pan) so rolls barely touch. Mix Coating ingredients. Brush over meat. Cover and cook on High (100% power) for 4-6 minutes, turning rolls after 3 minutes. Rolls should be firm when cooked. Stand 3-4 minutes in a warm place before serving.

Easy Beef Stew

For 4 servings:
600g cross-cut blade steak, pounded
1 pkt tomato soup
1 Tbsp flour
1 Tbsp worcestershire sauce
1 tsp dark soya sauce
¼ tsp thyme
1-2 cloves garlic, chopped
1 cup water or beer

Cut pieces of blade steak in half, remove and discard gristle. Pound with a meat hammer until thin. Place in casserole. Mix soup mix and flour. Sprinkle over meat. Add sauces, thyme and garlic and then the liquid. Cover and microwave on High (100% power) for 5 minutes, then at Defrost (30% power) for 45 minutes, or until meat is tender.

Beef and Vegetable Casserole

For 4 servings:
750g chuck or blade steak
¼ cup flour
2 tsp beef stock granules
2 tsp brown sugar
1 tsp paprika
¼ tsp thyme
2 onions, chopped
2 stalks celery, sliced
2 carrots, sliced thinly
1 bay leaf
1½ cups water
1 cup frozen peas
Dumplings (optional)
2 Tbsp chopped parsley

Cube steak. Mix with next 5 ingredients in a large casserole. Add vegetables and bay leaf. Mix again. Add hot tap water and stir well. Cover. Microwave on High (100% power) for 10 minutes, then at Defrost (30% power) for 1¼ hours or until meat is tender. Add peas after 45 minutes. In another dish make Dumplings if desired (See page 35). Add to stew and sprinkle with parsley.

Big Burgers

Neither my friends nor family like rare hamburgers. I add crumbs to my hamburgers because they keep the meat moist and juicy when cooked medium or well done.

Four burgers:
500g minced lamb or beef
1 thick slice bread, crumbled
1 Tbsp tomato ketchup
1 tsp dark soya sauce
2 tsp beef stock granules
2 spring onions, finely chopped

Combine all ingredients in the order given, until evenly mixed. Add a little milk if mixture seems firm. Cut mixture in four. Shape each quarter into a hamburger. Brush lightly with soya sauce.
To cook in browning dish: Heat browning dish for 6 minutes. Place burgers on hot surface. Cook on High (100% power).
For 2 burgers, cook 2 minutes, turn and cook 1-2 minutes more.
For 4 burgers, cook 2 minutes, turn and cook 3-4 minutes more.
Without a browning dish: Cook on High (100% power).
For 2 burgers, cook 2 minutes, turn and cook 2-3 minutes more.
For 4 burgers, cook 3 minutes, turn, and cook 3-4 minutes more.

Leave all burgers to stand 2-3 minutes after cooking.

Chilli Con Carne

Serve this on rice with a side salad, for a complete meal. If you want a crunchy accompaniment, add corn chips, crusty bread or crackers, too.

For 4-6 servings:
500g mince
2 medium onions, chopped
2 large cloves garlic, chopped
1/4 tsp chopped dried chillis (or 2 small dried chillis)
2 tsp oregano
1 tsp cumin
1 tsp paprika
1 can (420g) tomatoes in juice
1 large can (820g) baked beans in tomato sauce
1 green pepper, chopped

Combine the first 7 ingredients in a large uncovered casserole or bowl and microwave on High (100% power) for 5-7 minutes, stirring after each 2 minutes until meat is no longer pink. Add the tomatoes

and juice, beans and green pepper, cover and cook for a further 20 minutes, stirring occasionally. Serve in soup bowls on rice.
Note: this mixture is fairly hot! Use less chilli, if desired.

Spaghetti Sauce

For 6 servings:
500g minced beef
2 onions, chopped
2 cloves garlic, chopped
1 cup water
1 cup chopped or canned tomatoes in their own juice
1 pkt (3 serving size) tomato soup
1-2 red or green peppers, chopped
1 tsp celery or garlic salt
½ tsp dried basil
½ tsp dried marjoram
2 Tbsp tomato concentrate

Spread the minced beef, onion and garlic in a 23cm casserole dish and microwave uncovered on High (100% power) for 5-6 minutes, stirring once or twice. Add the water, tomatoes, tomato soup, peppers, flavoured salt and herbs, and tomato concentrate. Cover and microwave for 15 minutes, stirring once or twice during this time. Taste, adjust seasonings if necessary, and leave to stand for at least 5 minutes before serving.

Mushroom Mince

A special occasion, low-priced meat dish.

For 4-6 servings:
500g mince
2 cloves garlic, chopped
1 pkt mushroom soup
2 tsp mixed mustard
¾ cup water or white wine
1 Tbsp worcestershire sauce
4 spring onions, chopped
100g mushrooms, chopped
¼ cup sour cream or crème fraîche

In a large microwave casserole mix the mince and garlic and cook on High (100% power) for 5 minutes, stirring after 2 minutes. Add the soup, mustard, water or wine and the worcestershire sauce. Cook for another 6 minutes. Then add the spring onions and mushrooms and microwave for 2 minutes. Stir in the cream and serve over noodles or rice, or spoon onto toasted bread rolls.

Lazy Lasagne

For this family-style lasagne, nothing is precooked.

For 6 servings:
500g minced beef
2 cloves garlic, chopped
1 tsp dried basil
1 tsp dried oregano
1 can (425g) tomato purée
2 Tbsp tomato concentrate
1 pkt tomato soup
2 tsp beef stock granules
1½ cups hot water
150g (½pkt) lasagne noodles
2 cups grated cheese
2 tsp cornflour
1 egg
¾ cup milk
paprika

Mix first 9 ingredients thoroughly. Spray or butter a large ovenware dish which will turn in oven (23cm oval or round about 5cm deep). Pour ⅓ meat mixture into it. Place ½ lasagne pieces over meat, then sprinkle with ½ cup of the grated cheese. Layer another ⅓ of meat mixture, remaining lasagne and another ½ cup cheese. Cover with remaining meat. Cover dish and immediately microwave on High (100% power) for 30 minutes. Mix remaining cheese, egg, cornflour and milk. Pour over cooked mixture evenly, sprinkle with paprika, cover again and microwave on Medium (50% power) for 10 minutes or until topping sets. Leave to stand 15-30 minutes before cutting into squares (or reheat before serving later). Serve with salad.

Mini-Lasagne

This recipe makes a small lasagne which will cook in a rectangular 17 x 23cm or 20cm square dish with sides 3cm high.

For 3-4 servings:
250g minced lamb or beef
1 clove garlic, crushed
½ tsp basil
½ tsp oregano
1 cup tomato purée
1 Tbsp tomato concentrate
½ pkt tomato soup
1 tsp beef stock granules
1 cup hot water
100g lasagne noodles
1½ cups grated cheese
1 tsp cornflour
1 egg
½ cup milk
paprika

Follow method for Lazy Lasagne. Microwave on High (100% power) for 25 minutes, add topping and cook on Medium (50% power) for 10 minutes.

Note: If toppings do not set after specified times, reheat hot lasagne on High (100% power) for 2 minutes.

Oaty Meatballs

Meatballs microwave especially well. This basic meatball recipe has a good colour even before it is cooked, so you needn't worry that the colour of the final product will be in the least insipid.

For 4-5 servings:
500g minced beef or lamb
½ cup rolled oats
1 Tbsp beef or herb stock granules
1½ Tbsp dark soya sauce
2 Tbsp tomato ketchup
1 onion, grated or finely chopped
½ tsp dried basil
½ tsp dried majoram

Combine all the ingredients in a bowl or food processor. If using a food processor, chop the onion first, then add seasonings, the rolled oats and the meat. If mixture is too soft, add a little extra rolled oats. Divide mixture in quarters, then divide each quarter into eight walnut-sized balls. Arrange half of the meatballs in a circle round the edge of a large round flat dish. Meatballs should not be touching. Microwave, uncovered, on High (100% power) for 3-4 minutes. While first meatballs cook, shape the rest of the mixture into balls and cook in the same way.

Crumby Meatballs

These microwave very well. Added ingredients give colour, since they do not brown as much as conventionally cooked meatballs. They darken quite a lot in the 5 minutes after cooking, however.

For 4-5 servings:
250g minced lamb or beef
250g sausage meat
1 onion, finely chopped
1 cup soft breadcrumbs
1 Tbsp tomato ketchup
1 Tbsp dark soya sauce
1 egg
1½ tsp dried marjoram
¼ tsp dried thyme

Combine ingredients thoroughly in a bowl or food processor. Working with wet hands, divide mixture into quarters, then each quarter into 8-12 balls. Arrange half the balls in a circle around the edge of the turntable. Microwave on High (100% power) for 4 minutes or until firm. Remove, with juices. Cook remaining meatballs. Prepare and cook any suitable sauce, adding cooking juices from meatballs. Turn meatballs in sauce. Reheat and serve on rice, spaghetti, etc.

Glazed Meatloaf

Dress up a basic meatloaf! This cooks faster and more evenly in a ring mould, but you can use a traditional loaf pan if you like.

For 4-5 servings
500g minced beef or lamb
1 egg
1 onion, finely chopped
¼ cup tomato ketchup
1 Tbsp dark soya sauce
½ cup rolled oats
2 tsp beef stock granules
1 Tbsp tomato concentrate
2 Tbsp milk

Mix all of the ingredients above and pat into a small microwave ring mould. Cover with cling wrap and cook on Medium-High (70% power) for 12 minutes or High (100% power) for 9 minutes. Unmould onto serving dish. Drizzle glaze over surface.
Glaze:
¼ cup tomato sauce
2 tsp golden syrup
1 tsp worcestershire sauce
1 tsp dry mustard

For glaze, mix all ingredients in a small bowl, microwave on High (100% power) for 1 minute.

Steak and Chops

If you want to microwave steaks and chops regularly, you should buy a browning dish, since its use ensures the browned surface and slightly crusty texture of chops and steaks.

Before cooking, marinate chops, cutlets and steaks in a mixture of equal parts dark soya sauce, orange or lemon juice, and oil with 1-2 crushed garlic cloves.

If there is no time for this, brush the meat with dark soya sauce and a little oil before cooking.

In Browning Dish:
Preheat the browning dish according to manufacturer's instructions. Have meat at room temperature. Lay chops or steaks on the hot surface. Microwave on High (100% power).

For 2 chops or fillet steaks or 1 larger ribeye or striploin steak, cook 1 minute, turn, cook in microwave 1 minute longer. Leave in dish 2 minutes before serving.

For 4-6 chops, 4 fillet steaks or 2 large steaks cook 2 minutes, turn, cook 2 minutes longer. Leave to stand for 2-3 minutes.

Lift cooked chops or steaks from pan. Add 1-2 Tbsp of wine or vegetable liquid to browning dish. Stir to scrape brownings from bottom. Heat for 1-2 minutes, until liquid is reduced to 2-3 Tbsp. Add ½-1 tsp butter and swirl around pan. Pour over meat.

Without a Browning Dish
Marinate meat in marinade above or coat with soya sauce-oil mixture. Arrange chops or steaks, meatiest side out. Cover lightly with greaseproof paper. Cook on Medium (50% power). For each 2 chops or 1 steak cook for 2 minutes, drain off liquid, turn, cook 1-4 minutes longer, until cooked to the desired degree. Remove meat. Heat cooking juices on High (100% power) until they bubble and reduce. Pour over meat. Note: There are times when it is better to cook vegetables in a microwave oven while you pan-cook the meat!

Rolled Boneless Lamb Loin

For 4-6 servings:
1 loin of lamb (about 1kg after trimming), about 30cm long
1-2 tsp dark soya sauce
mixture of herbs and spices, e.g. mint, coriander, orange rind
3 kiwifruit, peeled

Bone and carefully trim the lamb leaving just enough fat to attach flap to meaty section. Rub both sides of meat with soya sauce. Sprinkle with flavourings to taste. Slice the kiwifruit and place slices in a line on top of the lamb, below the meatiest section. Roll up the lamb and secure with string. Cook on Medium (50% power) for 15-20 minutes or to internal temperature of 135°-145°F. Remove from oven and let stand about 8-10 minutes while you make the sauce.

Sauce:
1 orange, grated rind and juice
¼ cup red currant jelly
¼ cup meat juice (from cooked lamb)
2 tsp cornflour
1 Tbsp water

Blend the orange rind, juice and jelly by heating on High (100% power) for 2 minutes. Skim fat from meat juices and add to the mixture with the cornflour paste. Cook for 3 minutes until thickened. Serve sauce over the thickly sliced lamb. (See photograph on page 73.)

Pineapple Lamb Cutlets

For 4 servings:

8 lamb cutlets, well trimmed
(about 350g)
1 small can pineapple rings
2 Tbsp dark soya sauce
1 Tbsp tomato ketchup
1-2 Tbsp brown sugar
1 clove garlic
1 tsp freshly grated root ginger
2 tsp cornflour
halved circles of pineapple for
garnish

Trim the cutlets, removing all outer fat. In a shallow casserole or dish large enough to hold the cutlets in one layer, mix ¼ cup juice from the pineapple, the sauces, sugar, garlic and root ginger Turn cutlets in liquid. Leave to stand for at least 10 minutes. Turn again. Cover and microwave on Medium (50% power) for 12 minutes, turning after 6 minutes. Thicken with cornflour, mixed to a paste with a little extra pineapple juice. Stand for 4 minutes. Test. Cook 2-3 minutes or longer if meat is not quite cooked. Add halved pineapple rings to sauce. Coat with sauce. Reheat 1 minute on High (100% power) to heat pineapple. Serve with rice, noodles or mashed potatoes and colourful vegetables.

Creole Lamb Casserole

A one-step casserole which requires no last minute attention.

For 4-6 servings:
750g cubed shoulder lamb
¼ cup flour
2 tsp beef stock granules
1 tsp dry mustard
1 Tbsp Worcestershire sauce
2 tsp dark soya sauce
1 onion, chopped
1 green pepper, chopped
1 red pepper, chopped
2 cups chopped tomatoes (or 1 cup
tomato puree and 1 cup water)
about 10 drops hot pepper sauce

Trim lamb, removing fat, Toss meat with dry ingredients, then add remaining ingredients. Cook in a large, covered microwave dish on High (100% power) for 10 minutes, then stir and cook on Defrost (30% power) for 45 minutes or until meat is tender.

Tangy Pork Fillet

For 2-3 servings:
1 pork fillet (250-350g)
1 tsp dark soya sauce
1 tsp sesame oil
1 tsp sherry
1 clove garlic, chopped
Sauce:
2 tsp cornflour
1 tsp instant chicken stock
  granules
2 tsp dark soya sauce
¼ cup plum jam
¼ cup dry sherry
½ cup water
1 clove garlic, chopped

Cut fillet into pieces about 5mm thick. Mix with soya sauce, sesame oil, sherry and garlic. Leave to stand for at least 10 minutes. Cover and microwave on High (100% power) for 2-4 minutes, stirring after each minute until meat loses its pinkness. (Fillet can overcook in a very short time.) In another bowl combine sauce ingredients. Microwave, stirring occasionally, until smooth and clear.
Stir meat into cooked sauce and spoon over rice.

Pork and Pineapple

For 4 servings:
500g pork schnitzel, sliced
2 cloves garlic, chopped
2 tsp grated root ginger
2 Tbsp oil
2 onions, sliced
2 celery stalks, sliced
1-2 peppers, sliced (optional)
100g mushrooms, sliced
1 small can (225g) pineapple pieces
2 Tbsp cornflour
1 Tbsp brown sugar
2 Tbsp light soya sauce
1 tsp beef stock granules

Trim the schnitzel of excess fat and gristle. In a small bowl combine the pork, garlic, ginger and half the oil. Put aside. In casserole dish combine remaining oil, onions, celery and peppers. Cover and cook on High (100% power) for 5 minutes. Stir in meat mixture, mushrooms and drained pineapple pieces. Cover and cook 4 minutes or until pork is no longer pink. In empty bowl mix cornflour, brown sugar, sauce, stock granules and the juice from the pineapple made up to 1 cup with water or white wine. Heat until sauce thickens and boils,

stirring after 1 minute. Stir into casserole. Heat until sauce bubbles. Serve on rice or noodles.

Pork Spareribs

Rather messy finger food but deliciously addictive!

For 2-3 servings:
750g spareribs, cut into 2 ribs strips
1 cup boiling water
1 onion, chopped
1 stick celery, chopped

Place all ingredients in a covered casserole and microwave on High (100% power) for 5 minutes. Then cook a further 30-45 minutes on 30% power, until tender. Cover with Zesty Sauce before further cooking.

Zesty Sauce
1 Tbsp oil
1 onion, chopped
½ cup tomato ketchup
1 Tbsp brown sugar
1 tsp wine vinegar
1 tsp worcestershire sauce
dash of hot pepper sauce
¼ tsp garlic salt
½ tsp dry mustard

Combine the oil and onion in a bowl and microwave on High (100% power) for 2 minutes. Add the rest of the ingredients and cook 4 minutes or until thick. Lay the spareribs on flat plate in one layer. Spread half of the sauce on the ribs and cook uncovered for 2 minutes on Medium (50% power). Brush on the rest of the sauce and cook 2 minutes longer.
Note: If desired, crisp the surface under a grill just before serving.

Quick Curry

For 3 servings:
400g beef or pork schnitzel, sliced
2 cloves garlic, crushed
1 tsp grated root ginger
2 tsp lemon juice
2 tsp dark soya sauce
2 Tbsp butter or oil
1 large onion, chopped
2 tsp curry powder
¼ cup tomato relish
2 tsp brown sugar (optional)

Mix sliced meat, garlic, ginger, lemon juice and sauce. Leave to stand. Put butter or oil, onion and curry powder in a covered microwave dish. Cover and cook on High (100% power) for 5 minutes. Add tomato relish, stir and heat until bubbling, 2-3 minutes. Stir in meat, cover again and cook for 4 minutes, until meat loses its pinkness. Taste and add sugar if necessary. Thin sauce, if desired. Serve on rice.

Confetti Meatloaf

This mixture microwaves especially well and is popular hot or cold.

For 8-10 servings
500g mince
450g sausagemeat
1 onion, chopped
1 red pepper, chopped
1 green pepper, chopped
1 tsp curry powder
1 tsp herb stock granules
1 tsp beef stock granules
1 egg
1 cup fresh breadcrumbs
(about 2 slices bread)
about ½ cup Savoury Crumbs
or fine, dry breadcrumbs

Mix all except last ingredient. With wet hands, form mixture into a large, sausage shaped roll. Roll in Savoury or plain crumbs (see above) and place on a flat dish. Stand this on an inverted plate so that the meatloaf is raised from the bottom of the oven. Cook on 70% power for 20 minutes. Let stand for 5-8 minutes if serving hot, or leave to cool.
Variation:
Replace peppers with 1½ cups thawed mixed vegetables and up to 1 cup chopped celery, if desired.

Browned Sausages

Some skin-on sausages cook very well by this method, others don't. If necessary, brown them under a grill later, or add a topping of grated cheese and tomato ketchup or paprika for more colour.
Heat a browning dish according to manufacturer's instructions, about 6 minutes on High (100% power). Swirl 1 Tablespoon oil around the base. Add sausages (500g) which have been scored with parallel, diagonal cuts on both sides. Cook on High for 3 minutes, then turn sausages and cook 3 minutes longer, or until firm and cooked.

Devilled Sausage Patties

This topping adds flavour and colour.

500g sausage meat
Savoury Crumbs
2 tsp dry mustard
1 Tbsp worcestershire sauce
2 Tbsp tomato ketchup

few drops gravy browning (optional)

Form sausagemeat into 8 patties and turn in dry or Savoury Crumbs (page 16). Arrange in a circle on a flat plate. Mix together the mustard, worcestershire sauce, tomato and gravy browning. (The gravy browning gives a darker glaze.) Spread half of this mixture over the tops of the patties and microwave on High (100% power) for 3 minutes. Turn and brush or spread tops of patties with remaining mixture and cook 2-3 minutes, testing after 2 minutes to see if centres are cooked. Leave to stand 2-3 minutes before serving.

Sausagemeat

Inexpensive sausagemeat microwaves very well, although you do not get a crusty brown surface unless you use a browning dish.
To improve both the appearance and crispness of sausagemeat microwaved without a browning dish, you can use crumbs which have already been browned and crisped before being used to coat sausagemeat.

Savoury Crumbs

1 Tbsp butter
1 cup fresh breadcrumbs
1-2 Tbsp chopped parsley (optional)
1-2 tsp finely chopped herbs (optional)

Melt the butter in a fairly large, flat-bottomed microwave dish on High (100% power) for about 30 seconds. Add the breadcrumbs and finely chopped parsley and herbs if you want them for extra colour and flavour.
Spread the crumbs evenly, then cook for 2-4 minutes, until the crumbs turn golden brown. These crumbs make a good coating for any sausagemeat mixtures which are to be served without a sauce e.g. Confetti Meatloaf and Scotch Eggs (page 27). Country Terrine (page 31) is another good sausagemeat recipe.
If you find that your sausagemeat mixtures cook unevenly, lower the power level, increase the cooking time. Raise the cooking container by standing it on an inverted plate, or cover the food with a tent of greaseproof paper.

Saucy Sausages

Crumbed sausages don't brown as well in a microwave as they do in a frying pan, but they cook well. This tasty sauce improves both their colour and flavour.

For 4 servings:
8 crumbed sausages
1 Tbsp oil
2 Tbsp butter
2 medium onions, thinly sliced
2 medium apples, thinly sliced
1 tsp dry mustard
1 tsp beef stock granules
½ tsp celery salt
¼ cup brown sugar
2 tsp cornflour
2 Tbsp dark soya sauce
½ cup tomato ketchup
1 cup boiling water

Heat browning dish according to instructions. Make sure sausages are an even shape. (If crumbing them yourself, use Savoury Crumbs recipe, page 16). Add oil to hot browning dish. Add sausages, side by side. Cook on High (100% power) for 3 minutes, turn and cook 3 minutes longer. Remove from dish. If browning dish has sides and a lid, make sauce in it. Otherwise, use another dish. Put butter, onions and apples in a covered dish. Cook until tender, 4-6 minutes, stirring twice. While they cook, stir together dry ingredients, add sauces and boiling water. Pour over apple and onion and cover. Cook until thick and bubbly. Add sausages and reheat in sauce or serve over sausages.

Sausage and Mushroom Patties

Fast, easy and filling!
With wet hands, shape 8 patties from 500g sausage meat. Arrange in a circle on a large pyrex (or other suitable) round plate. Flatten the patties once they are on the plate, pushing them out with the heel of your hand until each one touches the patties beside it.

Microwave on High (100% power) for 4 minutes, then turn the patties over and pour over them a packet of mushroom sauce mix mixed with 1 cup of hot water and a few drops of gravy browning. Cook for 2 minutes longer.

Press the centre of each patty to see whether it is cooked. The patty will spring back if cooked, and will feel soft in the centre if it is still partly raw. If still uncooked, microwave for 1 minute more, then test again. When sausages are cooked, turn them in the sauce and leave to stand for several minutes. Sprinkle with chopped parsley and serve.

Roasting Meat

Tender meat cuts roast well in microwave ovens. use 50% power if time allows, otherwise 70% power. Only very tender cuts should be cooked at 100% power. Alter times accordingly.

* 50% power takes twice as long as 100% power.
* For 70% power, halve the difference and add it to the 100% power time.

    e.g. 8 minutes at 100% power
       16 minutes at 50% power
       12 minutes at 70% power

Fairly small compact roasts cook best. If roast is irregular or tapered, shield thin portions with foil to prevent them overcooking.
Roasts of marbled meat are more tender than lean roasts.
Trim fat to an even thin thickness. Meat close to fat (and close to surface bones) cooks faster. Excess fat can cause uneven cooking.
Turn meat at least once (preferably more) during cooking.
Estimate cooking time using weight of meat, but take shape into consideration, too. A long, thin roast cooks faster than a short, fat one of the same weight. For most accurate meat cookery, use a microwave meat thermometer. After experimenting, find what internal temperature you like meat cooked to, then always cook to this stage. Meat keeps cooking and its temperature keeps rising after it is taken from the oven. The thicker the meat, the greater the temperature rise, and the longer the standing time should be. Meat roasted rare or medium is more tender and juicy than meat which is cooked longer, to well done.

Important: Meat thermometer temperatures are often given in °Fahrenheit rather than °Celsius. Always roast meat on a rack or a raised plate, where it will not sit in a puddle of juice. If you do not have a rack, invert a bread and butter plate on a dinner plate. Remove meat juices as they accumulate since they slow down the cooking and may make it uneven.

In general, a piece of bone-in meat will cook more quickly than a boneless piece of the same weight. The microwave energy does not penetrate to the centre of a large roast. Thick pieces of meat cook fairly evenly to 5cm on all sides. The centre cooks by the transfer of heat, as in conventional roasts.

Making Gravy

It's worth taking a little time and effort to make gravy to serve with roast meat. If you are making gravy from light coloured meat drippings, you will probably want to add some colouring. Make the gravy in a measure jug, or in the jug in which you will serve the gravy.

Make a well flavoured stock by heating together in a bowl 1 teaspoon instant stock granules, 1½ cup water, any meat trimmings, bones or giblet, and a selection of finely chopped vegetables and herbs. Include onion skins and mushrooms to darken colour, if possible.
Microwave on High (100% power) for 5 minutes, then on Defrost (30% power) for 15 minutes.
Put 2-3 tablespoons of fat from pan drippings or 2 tablespoons of butter in a measuring jug or gravy boat. Melt if necessary. Stir in 3 tablespoons of flour and mix well.
Microwave on High (100% power) until mixture turns light brown. Add the stock from the vegetables, stirring all the time. Add remaining pan drippings, with fat skimmed off. Microwave on High until gravy bubbles, then remove and stir until smooth.
If gravy still looks light, add a few drops of gravy browning. Season to taste.

Roast Beef

I find that tender roasts of beef up to 1½kg microwave very well at Medium (50% power). Large roasts or tougher, rolled roasts I prefer to cook conventionally. For successful tender roasts for 3-6 people, choose a roast from the rib eye (sometimes called Scotch fillet or Cube Roll) or the boneless loin (or striploin or sirloin). For a small roast for 2-3 people, ask for the triangular tip or the last cut from the rump (less expensive), or the fillet (most tender and most expensive). Trim any thick pieces of fat from meat, leaving an even coating. Tie meat in several places if you want round, compact slices; otherwise, leave it untied. Weigh meat to estimate approximate cooking time. Make a paste of equal parts of dry mustard and dark soya sauce and rub the sides (not the ends) of the meat with it, if desired. Stand meat on a ridged or elevated roasting pan, fat side down. Estimate cooking time, turn after half the time.

Cook on Medium (50% power) allowing

Rare	10-13 min. per 500g
Medium	14-16 min. per 500g
Well Done	18-20 min. per 500g

	Internal temp when cooked	Internal temp after standing
Rare	125°F (50°C)	145°F (62°C)
Medium	135°-140°F (60°C)	150°F (65°C)
Well Done	145°-150°F (65°C)	160°F (70°C)

Beef will be more tender when cooked rare or medium. Well done meat will be drier and tougher. The photograph shows a boneless loin roast, cooked to 135°F. If time is short, cook on Medium-High (70% power) and reduce cooking times accordingly.

Roast Pork

1-1½kg rolled shoulder or loin of pork with outer fat and skin removed
dark soya sauce (optional)

Have butcher remove skin and outer fat before rolling pork. Weigh to estimate approximate roasting time. Rub surface with soya sauce, if desired. Place roast on ridged or raised roasting pan, fat side down. Cover loosely. Cook at Medium (50% power), allowing 15-20 minutes per 500g. Turn meat after 20-30 minutes. Internal temperature should be 155°F (68°C). Remove meat and stand in a warm place for 15 minutes.

Temperature will rise to 170°F (77°C).
Skim juices and thicken to make gravy.

Shoulder of Lamb

For 4 servings:
1 shoulder of lamb, boned
2 Tbsp mixed mustard
1 Tbsp dark soya sauce
1 tsp chopped fresh thyme

Trim all excess fat from surface and inner, meaty side of boned lamb shoulder. Score outer skin in a diamond pattern with a sharp knife. In a small bowl, mix the mustard, soya sauce and thyme to a spreadable paste, and brush over both surfaces of the meat. Roll up, skin side out, and tie securely in several places. Place the lamb on a microwave roasting rack (or substitute, see page 70). Cover with a tent of greaseproof paper. Microwave on Medium (50% power) allowing 20-25 minutes per 500g. Turn lamb, every 10-15 minutes. Allow 10 minutes standing time. Slice and serve with gravy made by skimming, then reducing or thickening pan juices.

Bagged Stuffed Lamb

For 4-6 servings:
1 boned trimmed lamb leg
1 large onion, chopped finely
1 Tbsp oil
¼ cup chopped apricots
½ cup Australian raisins
¼ cup chopped walnuts
¼ cup sherry or orange juice
2-3 Tbsp chopped mint
Marinade:
2 Tbsp dark soya sauce
2 Tbsp sherry or orange juice
2 Tbsp lemon juice
1 clove garlic, crushed

In a medium-sized bowl combine the onion and oil. Microwave on High (100% power) for 1 minutes. Add the apricots, raisins and walnuts and sherry. Cook, uncovered for 3 minutes. Stir in the mint. Place this mixture on the meaty surface of the boned leg. Roll up and tie securely with string. (Skewers may puncture oven bag.) Place stuffed leg in an oven bag with the marinade ingredients, closed loosely with a rubber band, leaving a finger-sized hole. Microwave on medium (50% power) allowing 15-20 minutes per 500g. Turn after 15 minutes. For slightly pink lamb the internal temperature of the meat should be 135F before standing. Pour off liquid, skim off fat and thicken with cornflour paste. Leave meat to stand for 10 minutes. Slice, garnish with fresh herbs and serve.

Roast Leg of Lamb

I microwave legs of small, young lamb but roast older lamb and hogget conventionally. Over-cooked lamb is sometimes tough, so it is best cooked-medium, rather than well-done.

1 leg of young lamb, shank
*   removed*
garlic (optional)
fresh rosemary (optional)
2 tsp mixed mustard
2 tsp dark soya sauce

Trim away thick pieces of fat so meat has an even, thin fat covering. Weigh and estimate approximate cooking time. Insert slivers of garlic and leaves of rosemary in small cuts in flesh, if desired. Rub surface with paste made from mixing mustard and soya sauce. Shield

shank end of leg with an 8cm strip of foil.

Place meat on a ridged or raised roasting pan. Cook on High (100% power) for 5 minutes, then on Medium (50% power) for 10-15 minutes per 500g, turning meat over after 20 minutes and removing the foil.

Cook until meat thermometer registers 140-150°F (60-65°C) depending on whether medium or well done meat is wanted. Cover and leave to stand in a warm place for 10 minutes, covered with a tent of foil.

To Make Gravy: Skim pan juices, thicken with cornflour, baste and season as desired.

Roast Lamb Rack

This is my favourite small roast. The meat is so tender it may be cooked on High (100% power) in a very short time.

For 2-3 servings:
*1 chined frenched lamb rack, with
   8 chops (400-500g)
1 Tbsp mixed mustard
1 tsp dark soya sauce
2 Tbsp parmesan cheese
2 Tbsp dry breadcrumbs
½ tsp paprika
1-2 Tbsp chopped fresh herbs,
   optional*

Trim the outer layer of skin and fat from a chined frenched rack by running your thumb between the rib eye muscle and its outer fat coating. When this muscle is nearly exposed, cut with a sharp knife down to the bones, then lift and cut away the remaining fat. Trim rib bones shorter, if required. (Diagonal cutting pliers do this job well and may be used to chine the rack if necessary.)

Brush all meaty surface with a paste made by mixing the mustard and soya sauce. Mix crumbs, cheese, paprika and chopped herbs and sprinkle over mustard. Stand on ridged or elevated roasting pan, meaty side up.

Microwave rack (weighing 400g or less after trimming) on High (100% power) for 4½ minutes. Add an extra 30 seconds per extra 50g. Leave to stand 5 minutes, then carve into cutlets. Serve with pan juices. For an alternative coating: Spread roast with a paste of 1 Tbsp mixed mustard and 2-3 tsp dark soya sauce. Pat ¼ cup chopped parsley and mixed herbs over it.

Whole Chickens

Whole chickens cook well and quickly in microwave ovens.

Defrosting:
Defrost chickens at 20% or 30% power levels for about 30 minutes. Always defrost frozen chickens before cooking them at higher power levels. Remove commercial wrappings and metal clips. Place bird in a bag (unless using automatic function and other instructions). During thawing, turn chicken, pour off accumulating liquid, loosen joints, remove giblets and internal ice, and mask with small pieces of foil any parts that are overcooking (see page 13). After thawing, centre should be cold but not icy.

Note:
Microwave defrosting is convenient when time is limited. When possible, however, thaw chicken at room temperature for several hours, or in refrigerator overnight. For chicken which will be marinated before cooking, thaw in marinade, if desired.

Coatings and Marinades:
Because chicken skin does not brown much during cooking, it is usually coated with a mixture which will add colour as well as flavour. Use any of the coatings for chicken pieces, on pages 76 and 77 or try the following recipes.

Bags and Covers:
Whole chickens cook more quickly, and more evenly, if they are enclosed as they cook. Oven bags produce excellent results, with the chicken skin losing its 'steamed' appearance soon after it is removed from the bag after cooking. Casseroled chickens cook well, and have the same appearance and texture as those casseroled in conventional ovens. When microwaving chickens, uncovered, you should cover them loosely with a tent of baking paper or greaseproof paper, since this helps the bird cook more evenly and quickly.

Bagged Roast Chicken

This chicken gains colour from its marinade.

2 Tbsp dark soya sauce
2 Tbsp sherry
2 Tbsp worcestershire sauce
1 Tbsp honey
1 clove garlic, crushed or chopped

Mix marinade ingredients in an unpunctured oven bag. If necessary, heat marinade in bag to soften and dissolve honey. Add chicken to bag with marinade. Remove air from bag so marinade surrounds chicken. Fasten with rubber band. Turn occasionally. Leave to stand for at least an hour, but longer if desired.
Before cooking, loosen rubber band, leaving a finger-sized hole so steam can escape during cooking. For preference, microwave on 70% power, allowing 10 minutes per 500g. If necessary, roast on High (100% power) for 8 minutes per 500g.
After standing for 5 minutes after cooking, the flesh between leg and breast should no longer look pink. When cooking a large chicken, turn it several times during cooking for most even results and best colour.

Roast Chicken

For good colour glaze chicken before (and during) cooking with a mixture of:

2 Tbsp melted butter and
1 Tbsp dark soya sauce

To make sure glaze colours chicken evenly, first scrub the skin with warm water and a soft brush. Pat dry, then brush with butter and soya sauce mixture.
Place chicken, breast side down, on rack in roasting pan or on ridged baking pan. Cover with a tent of greaseproof paper. Microwave on High (100% power) for 10-15 minutes, depending on size of chicken, then on Medium (50% power) for 12 minutes per 500g. Turn chicken breast side up after half the estimated cooking time. Brush with more glaze if desired. Leave to stand for 10 minutes. When cooked, leg should move freely. Flesh between leg and breast should no longer be pink.
The bird photographed is a "grand poulet" weighing 2kg.

Forcemeat Balls

If you like stuffing, cook these balls during the chicken's standing time and serve alongside the chicken.

450-500g sausagemeat
½ cup soft breadcrumbs
½ cup crushed pineapple
1 onion, finely chopped
2 Tbsp chopped parsley
1 tsp fresh thyme
½ tsp salt
Savoury Crumbs (see page 16)
*   or fine dry crumbs*

Mix first seven ingredients until well blended. Form into 12-16 balls with wet hands. Roll in Savoury or dry crumbs. Arrange in a circle on a flat plate or on the turntable. Microwave on High (100% power) for 5 minutes, or until firm.

Microwaving Chicken Pieces

Chicken pieces microwave wonderfully well, very quickly. They are tender and juicy, with an excellent flavour. If you start with frozen chicken pieces, you should always defrost them first, before coating and cooking them.

To Defrost: Wrap in greaseproof paper, or arrange in a covered container in one layer, thickest part out, or place in one layer in an oven bag and defrost on 20% or 30% power, allowing 2-3 minutes per piece.

Chicken pieces do not brown or become crisp in the short cooking time needed, so you should use coatings which add colour and crispness as well as flavour.

For most even cooking, select one cut, rather than a mixture, e.g. drumsticks or thighs.

To cook coated chicken pieces, pat chicken pieces dry with paper towels. Coat chicken pieces with melted butter or oil (or dip in an egg coating). Shake in plastic bag with coating mixture, or turn in shallow bowl of coating. Arrange on a ridged dish or on a flat plate with meatiest side towards edge of dish with the skin side (best looking side) uppermost. Cover loosely with a paper towel, or leave uncovered. Cook on High (100% power) for 2-3 minutes per piece, allowing about 10 minutes per 500g.

If dish is crowded, move chicken positions after half the estimated time, but do not turn the pieces over. Leave 2 minutes before testing to see whether pieces are ready.

When cooked, juices should run clear, not pink, and flesh near bone should not be pink.

Paprika Baked Chicken

For 8-12 pieces:
First coating
melted butter
Second coating
¼ cup flour
2 tsp paprika
1 tsp curry powder
2 tsp garlic salt
2 tsp castor sugar

Brush chicken pieces with butter and lay on plastic or greaseproof paper, skin side down. Combine ingredients for second coating in a jar with an airtight lid.
Tip some of the second coating into a fine sieve. Coat chicken thickly, then turn pieces over and shake coating over skin side. Arrange on baking dish, skin side up. Cook as for coated chicken pieces.
Note: Keep remaining coating for later use.

Herbed Crumbed Chicken

First coating
1 tsp garlic salt
½ tsp paprika

¼ tsp curry powder
1 Tbsp water
1 egg
Second coating
25g butter, melted
2 cups soft breadcrumbs
2 Tbsp chopped parsley

Prepare second coating by melting butter on High (100% power) for about 50 seconds. Stir in breadcrumbs and parsley (or other fresh herbs, or smaller amounts of dried herbs to taste). Heat on a flat dish for about 3 minutes or until golden brown, stirring after every minute.
Mix first coating. Add garlic salt, paprika and curry powder to water. Stir to mix. Add egg and beat with a fork, just enough to combine white, yolk and seasonings.
Turn dried chicken pieces first in the egg dip, then in the crumbs. Place chicken directly on a baking dish, skin side up, thicker pieces near the edge. Cook as for coated chicken pieces.
Note: Keep leftover crumbs for later use. For thicker coating, dip chicken in flour before other coatings.

Teriyaki Chicken

For 4 chicken pieces:
Marinade:
2 Tbsp dark soya sauce
2 Tbsp medium or dry sherry
1 Tbsp brown sugar
1 tsp garlic salt
2 tsp grated root ginger or
  1 tsp ground ginger
½ tsp cornflour

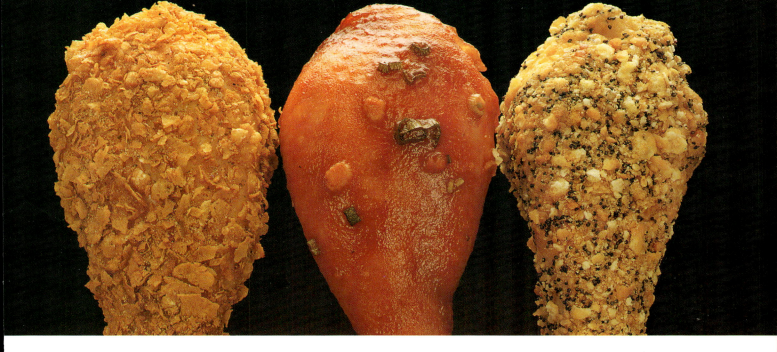

Put chicken pieces in an unpunctured oven bag with all marinade ingredients. Remove air from bag and fasten tightly with a rubber band. Leave to stand for 30 minutes to 1 hour if possible, turning occasionally.

Loosen rubber band, leaving a finger-sized hole. Position bag so it is flat, with chicken pieces in one layer, with thicker parts near the outside. Cook as for coated chicken pieces, turning bag once during cooking time, so chicken is evenly coated.

While still very hot, turn pieces in sauce and remove from the bag. Coating dries on standing a few minutes.

Golden Crusted Chicken

For about 6 chicken pieces
First coating
1 tsp celery salt
¹⁄₂ tsp paprika
¹⁄₄ tsp curry powder
1 Tbsp milk
1 egg
Second coating
1 cup crushed cornflakes

Mix first coating. Add celery salt, paprika and curry powder to milk. Stir to mix. Add egg and beat with a fork, just enough to combine. Crush cornflakes in a food processor or in a plastic bag with a rolling pin. Turn dried chicken pieces, first in the seasoned egg, then in the crushed crumbs. Place on baking dish, skin side up, thicker pieces near the edge. Cook as for coated chicken pieces.

Note: Keep leftover crumbs for later use.

Barbecued Chicken

First coating
flour
Second coating
2 Tbsp brown sugar
1 tsp dry mustard
¹⁄₂ tsp garlic salt
2 tsp cornflour
1 tsp worcestershire sauce
1 Tbsp tomato concentrate
¹⁄₂ cup tomato ketchup
basil and marjoram (optional)

Dip chicken pieces first in flour, then brush with second coating made by mixing together the barbecue sauce ingredients in the order given. Add herbs as desired. Cook as for coated chicken pieces. Coating dries on standing a few minutes.

Cracker-Crusted Chicken

For about 6-8 pieces:
First coating
1 tsp onion or garlic salt
¹⁄₂ tsp paprika
¹⁄₄-¹⁄₂ tsp curry powder
1 Tbsp milk
1 egg
Second coating
¹⁄₂ cup crushed golden-brown coloured crackers
1 Tbsp toasted sesame seeds
1 Tbsp poppy seeds

Mix first coating. Add flavoured salt, paprika and curry powder to milk. Stir to mix. Add egg and beat with a fork, just enough to combine. Mix cracker crumbs with the seeds. Dip dried chicken pieces first in the seasoned egg, then in the cracker crumb mixture. Place on baking dish, skin side up, thicker pieces near the edge. Cook as for coated chicken pieces.

Note: Keep leftover crumbs for later use if not damp.

Devilled Drumsticks

For two servings:
4 chicken drumsticks
1 Tbsp mixed mustard
¹⁄₂ tsp garlic salt
2 tsp worcestershire sauce
1 Tbsp parmesan cheese
¹⁄₄ tsp paprika

Mix mustard, garlic salt and worcestershire sauce. Brush on chicken. Sprinkle with mixed parmesan cheese and paprika. Bake uncovered as for coated chicken pieces, about 8 minutes. Serve hot or cold.

Glazed Chicken Breasts

Chicken breasts toughen if overcooked. Take care!

For 4 servings:
4 chicken breasts
flour
2 Tbsp white wine or apple juice
2 tsp soya sauce
2 tsp worcestershire sauce
1 clove garlic, chopped
1 Tbsp chives or spring onion
  leaves

Place chicken breasts between two sheets of plastic. Pound gently with rolling pin until flattened. Sprinkle lightly with flour on both sides. Measure remaining ingredients into dish large enough to hold chicken in one layer. Turn chicken pieces in liquid. Cover and cook at High (100% power) for 7-8 minutes, turning after 4 minutes. Stand 2-3 minutes. Flesh should not be pink or translucent when cooked.

Crunchy Chicken Rolls

Quickly cooked chicken for a special occasion.

Savoury Crumbs (see page 16)
4 chicken breasts
50g butter
1 rasher bacon, chopped
½ cup finely chopped mushrooms
1 Tbsp soft breadcrumbs
¼ cup flour
1 egg, beaten

First make Savoury Crumbs. Next pound chicken breasts between two layers of plastic until thin. To make stuffing, melt butter in a small container. Add 1 Tbsp of the melted butter to the bacon, mushrooms and soft breadcrumbs and mix. Cover and cook on High (100% power) for 3 minutes, stirring or shaking after 1 minute. Put a pile of stuffing on the inner side of each breast. Roll up and secure with toothpicks. Dust lightly with flour, then turn first in beaten egg to coat, then in the Savoury Crumbs. Arrange in a circle on a flat dish. Pour remaining melted butter over them and bake, uncovered, for 8 minutes. Stand 2-3 minutes before serving.

Stir-Fried Chicken

A stir-fried taste, without any spatters.

For 4 servings:
400g chicken breasts or other boneless chicken meat
3 Tbsp oil
1 Tbsp light soya sauce
1 Tbsp sherry
2 tsp brown sugar
2 tsp chicken stock granules
2 tsp cornflour
1 clove garlic, chopped
1 tsp grated root ginger
400g quick cooking vegetables, sliced

Cut chicken into 5mm slices, discarding skin. Place in oven bag with 1 Tbsp oil and all ingredients, except vegetables. Knead to mix and leave to marinate. Slice vegetables into thin slices. Coat with remaining oil. Stir-fry vegetables in covered casserole on High (100% power) for 4 minutes. Leave to stand. Spread bag containing chicken so it is flat. Fasten bag with rubber band, leaving finger-sized hole. Microwave 3-4 minutes. Leave to stand for 1 minute. Chicken should be milky white. Stir chicken into vegetables and serve immediately on rice.

Mushroom Chicken

Chicken breasts in an easy creamy sauce.

For 4 servings:
4 chicken breasts
1 Tbsp butter
½ tsp paprika
6-8 small mushrooms, sliced
1 tsp cornflour
½ tsp garlic salt
¼ cup cream
2 Tbsp chopped parsley

Pat chicken breasts dry. Melt butter in dish large enough to hold chicken in one layer. Turn in butter. Sprinkle lightly with a little of the paprika. Slice mushrooms thinly over chicken. Cover and microwave on High (100% power) for 6 minutes.
Reposition chicken if necessary. Mix cornflour, garlic salt, cream and remaining paprika. Pour over chicken. Sprinkle with parsley. Bake uncovered for 2-3 minutes, then stand 2-3 minutes. Meat should not be pink or translucent. Pour juices over chicken again. Serve.
Note: Use chicken thighs if preferred.

Chicken Breast for One

You can coat and cook this in a very short time.

1 chicken breast
flour
1 tsp butter
1 tsp worcestershire sauce
1 tsp white wine or lemon juice
2 tsp chopped parsley
paprika

Dry chicken breast. Pound between two pieces of plastic to flatten, if desired. Coat lightly with flour, patting it in well. In a small dish melt butter for 20 seconds on High (100% power). Turn chicken in melted butter, then in the sauce and wine or juice. Sprinkle with parsley and paprika. Cover and cook:
1 min 45 sec at High (100% power)
or 2 min at Medium-High (70% power)
or 3 min at Medium (50% power)

Lemon Chicken

A tangy sauce coats chunks of tender breast meat.

For 2 servings:
2 chicken breasts
1 tsp sherry
1 clove garlic (optional)
1 Tbsp oil
½ tsp grated root ginger
1 red pepper
1 green pepper
2-3 spring onions
Sauce
2 tsp cornflour
1 Tbsp sugar
½ tsp chicken stock granules
¼ cup water
1 Tbsp sherry
2 Tbsp lemon juice

Preheat browning dish for 6 minutes. Cut each chicken breast into 5 or 6 crosswise slices. Mix with sherry, garlic, oil and ginger.

Cut peppers into pieces about the same size as the chicken. Cut spring onions into 1cm lengths. Mix sauce ingredients in a cup. Add chicken and vegetables to hot browning dish. Stir briefly. Microwave on High (100% power) for 1 minute. Add sauce, stir briefly, and cook 30 seconds or until sauce thickens and until chicken is cooked.
DO NOT OVERCOOK. Serve on rice.
Variation: Add ½ tsp sesame oil to chicken marinade.

Tricky Take-aways

Dress up a cooked chicken for a speedy meal.

For 4 servings:
1 cooked chicken, jointed
2 cloves garlic
2 tsp butter
½ tsp paprika

1 tsp lemon juice
1 tsp green herbs stock granules
1 tsp cornflour
½ cup white wine

Divide barbecued chicken into two leg and two breast and wing pieces, removing unnecessary bones. Chop garlic finely. Mix with remaining ingredients in a casserole large enough to hold chicken in one layer. Heat sauce 2 minutes, until it thickens and boils. Brush over all chicken surfaces. Place chicken, skin side up, in remaining sauce. Cover lightly and reheat when needed, 5-10 minutes on Medium-High (70% power).

Curried Pineapple Chicken

This couldn't be easier to prepare and cook!

For 4 servings:
4 chicken legs
1 pkt cream of chicken or onion soup mix
1-2 tsp curry powder
1 can (400g) pineapple slices or pieces
1-2 tsp dark soya sauce

Halve chicken legs for easier mixing, cooking and serving. Shake in oven bag with the dry soup mix and curry powder. Drain liquid from pineapple. Make up to 1¼ cups with water. Add to chicken with soya sauce, kneading bag gently to mix well. Secure bag with a rubber band, leaving a finger-sized opening. Lay bag flat on a dinner plate so chicken pieces are in one layer. Microwave on High (100% power) for 12 minutes, turning bag after 8 minutes. Add pineapple pieces, circles or half circles. Cook 2-3 minutes longer. Test to see that chicken juice is clear, not pink. Serve.

Orange Chicken

Mix and cook in a bag for a no mess, no wash-up main course.

For 4 servings:
4 chicken legs
1 Tbsp brown sugar
1 Tbsp cornflour
1 Tbsp tomato ketchup
1-2 cloves garlic, sliced
1 tsp dark soya sauce
¼ tsp grated nutmeg
½ cup orange juice

Halve chicken legs for easier mixing and serving. Put in oven bag with brown sugar and cornflour. Shake to coat. Add remaining ingredients in order given, kneading bag gently to mix. Secure bag with a rubber band, leaving a finger-sized opening. Lay bag flat on a dinner plate so chicken pieces are in one layer. Microwave on High (100% power) for 15 minutes, turning bag over after 8 minutes. Leave to stand 5 minutes, knead bag again to mix, then serve.

Chicken Fricasee

Smoked chicken is already cooked when you buy it. It reheats deliciously in this sauce.

For 4 servings:
200g carrots
1 cup sliced celery
4 small onions
50g butter
¾ cup water
2 Tbsp flour
1 tsp green herbs stock granules
1 cup milk
2 cups smoked chicken or cooked chicken
½-1 cup peas

Slice carrots thinly. Cook with celery and quartered onions in the butter, with ¼ cup water, in a covered casserole on High (100% power) for 8 minutes, until vegetables are tender. Stir in flour and stock granules, then the milk and remaining water. Cook, uncovered until sauce boils and thickens, stirring every minute. Add chicken and peas, heat 2 minutes longer and serve with rice or mashed potatoes.

Vegetables

Vegetables

Microwaved vegetables have excellent colour, flavour, texture and vitamin content. Salt is not added before cooking.
Experiment with small additions of water, oil or butter, and different vegetable combinations, to find your favourites.
For most vegetables (and mixtures) use the following general method (see picture opposite).

Allow about 100g prepared vegetable per serving.
Wash, then slice or cut as you would for stir-frying. Cut quicker cooking vegetables in larger pieces than slower cooking ones.

For each serving heat ½-1 tsp butter or oil with ½ finely sliced garlic clove in the cooking container. Add prepared vegetable and toss to coat evenly.
Add 1 tsp water per serving for soft-textured vegetables. Add none for tender-crop vegetables.
Cover tightly. Microwave on High (100% power).
Allow 1-2 minutes for 1 serving
    1½-3 minutes for 2 servings
    2½-4 minutes for 3 servings
    3-5 minutes for 4 servings

Allow 2 minutes standing time.

Some vegetables need no wrapping because their skin holds in moisture.
Always puncture or cut skins before cooking.

Cut, sliced or chopped vegetables should be covered during cooking so that they cook in steam. Add salt and pepper after cooking, only if necessary.

Oven bags are very useful for cooking vegetables. Close bags loosely with rubber bands, leaving an unobstructed finger-sized hole for steam and air to escape.

When cooking vegetables in dishes that have no lids, cover with plastic cling wrap, folding back one edge or piercing plastic so that steam can escape during cooking.

Vegetables for one serving may be cooked in a double layered parcel of greaseproof paper, Paper cannot be used for large quantities or long cooking.

Small quantities of frozen vegetables can be cooked in the sealed plastic bags in which they are bought. Always pierce bag before cooking.

Cut vegetables into small, even pieces before microwaving. Large pieces of hard vegetables, require much longer cooking than small pieces.

Stir or shake containers of vegetables, especially larger quantities, several times during cooking, so food in the centre will cook more quickly and evenly.

Vegetables may not appear ready after cooking (left) but finish cooking during standing time (right).

Potatoes

You and your microwave can make the humble potato into the high point of your meal, in a shorter time than you would imagine possible!
Potatoes cook fastest in a container just big enough to hold them. An oven bag produces fastest results.
Undercooked potatoes are hard. Overcooked potatoes are shrunken.

Baked Potatoes

Scrub large potatoes. Prick each potato 4-6 times. Turn potatoes half way through the estimated cooking time.
At the end of the cooking time they should feel softish, but not completely cooked. They continue cooking during 2 minute standing time.
Mark a cross with a fork or knife. Press down, towards the centre, so cross opens out.
Top with butter, sour cream, yoghurt, cream, hard or soft cheese, blue cheese, mustard pickle etc. Melt or heat topping briefly, if desired.
Garnish with parsley and/or paprika and serve.
Baking times at High (100% power).
1 small potato (100g) 3 min.
2 med. potatoes (300g) 7-8 min.
3 med. potatoes (400g) 10 min.
4 large potatoes (600-800g) 12-14 min.

Stuffed Potatoes

Bake large potatoes (see previous recipe).
Halve potatoes or cut off tops.

Scoop out most of the flesh. Mash until smooth and creamy, adding butter, cream cheese, mayonnaise, sour cream or yoghurt.
Add desired filling ingredients, season carefully, and pile filling back into shells. Reheat, allowing 1-2 minutes per potato.
Suitable fillings include — grated cheese, spring onion, sautéed onion, peppers, mushrooms, or bacon, garlic, creamed corn, baked beans, pickles, chutneys, herbs, smoked fish, cooked mince and pâté, and combinations of above.

Mashed Potato

Make sure potatoes are not overcooked or undercooked when you prepare these.

For 4 servings
4 medium-large potatoes
¼ cup water
1 Tbsp butter
milk
salt and pepper

Select a bowl in which potatoes can be cooked, mashed and served. Half fill bowl with cold water. Peel potatoes, halve each lengthwise, then cut each half into 4-6 fairly even, fairly square pieces. When all are prepared, drain off water.
Add butter and water. Cover. Microwave on High (100% power) for 7-10 minutes. Shake after 4-5 minutes, to coat with melted butter and to reposition.
Test with sharp knife, removing potatoes as soon as centre cubes are tender.
Leave to stand for 4-5 minutes, or until potatoes are required, then mash, adding milk, salt and pepper to taste. Beat mashed potatoes with a fork, after mashing.

New Potatoes

New potatoes cook beautifully in a microwave oven!
Scrub potatoes, scraping them if desired, halve or quarter large potatoes, or peel a ring of skin from around the middle of small whole potatoes. Drop into a cold water as they are prepared, to stop them browning. Just before cooking, transfer to a microwave casserole, or oven bag. Add 1 Tbsp water per serving and a mint sprig and ½ tsp butter per serving. Cover or close bag loosely.

Approximate cooking times on High (100% power):
1 serving (100-125g) 2½ minutes
2 servings (200-250g) 3½-4 minutes
4 servings (400-500g) 5½-6 minutes

Shake casserole or turn bag half way through cooking time. Potatoes are cooked when barely tender. Allow standing time of 3-4 minutes.

Plain Potatoes

These cook fastest in an oven bag. Scrub or thinly peel the potatoes. Halve or quarter large ones. Place in an oven bag. Add 2 tsp water per serving. Fasten bag loosely.

Approximate cooking times on High (100% power):
1 serving (125-150g) 3 min.
2 servings (250-300g) 4½-5 min.
4 servings (500-600g) 6-8 min.

Turn bag half way through estimated time. Cooked potatoes give slightly when pressed. Allow standing time of 5 minutes.

Golden Potatoes

These are cooked in a preheated browning dish for a crispy surface.

For 2 servings
2 medium potatoes
1 Tbsp flour
1 tsp salt
1 tsp paprika
½ tsp curry powder
1 Tbsp butter or oil

Preheat browning dish for 6 minutes. Scrub or peel potatoes. Cut into small (1cm) cubes. Shake in plastic bag with the next four ingredients, to coat evenly. Add butter to heated browning dish. Quickly spread coated potatoes on hot buttered surface. Microwave on High (100% power) for 3 minutes. Turn. Cook 2-3 minutes longer, or until tender.

Savoury Potatoes

For 4 servings
3 fairly large potatoes (500g)
2 onions, sliced
1 clove garlic
25g butter
100g mushrooms, sliced
½ tsp salt
2 spring onions, chopped
paprika

Scrub or peel and slice potatoes. Combine onions, finely chopped garlic and butter in a shallow casserole dish. Cover and microwave on High (100% power) for 2 minutes.
Add potatoes and mix evenly. Cover and cook 6-7 minutes, until barely tender.
Add mushrooms, cover and cook 2 minutes longer. Stand for 2

minutes, then toss gently with the salt, spring onions and paprika.

Scalloped Potatoes

(see cover photo)

For 2 servings
2-3 medium potatoes
1 small-medium onion
1 clove garlic
2 tsp butter
1 Tbsp water
1 Tbsp flour
½ cup milk
flavoured salt
½ cup grated cheese
parsley and paprika

Scrub potatoes. Slice thinly into a shallow casserole dish (about 20cm across) with thinly sliced onion and finely chopped garlic between layers of potato. Add butter and water, cover, and cook on High (100% power) for 5 minutes until barely tender, shaking dish after 2-3 minutes. Sprinkle potatoes with flour then add milk.
Sprinkle with a little celery, onion, or garlic salt. Cover and cook again until sauce thickens.
Sprinkle surface with grated cheese, chopped parsley and paprika. Microwave, uncovered, until cheese melts, about 1 minute.

Grated Potato Cake

4 potatoes
25g butter
1 or 2 cloves garlic
2 tsp powdered stock granules
¼ cup chopped spring onion
or finely chopped parsley
½-1 cup grated cheese
parsley and paprika

Scrub potatoes and grate coarsely. Heat butter and finely chopped garlic in small ring pan.
Rinse potatoes with cold water and drain thoroughly in sieve.
Mix with melted butter, green herbs or chicken stock granules and spring onion or parsley in a large mixing bowl.
Press evenly and lightly into ring pan. Cover with vented plastic film. Microwave on High (100% power) for 10 minutes, or until potato is tender.
Leave 2 minutes, then turn onto flat plate. Sprinkle evenly with cheese, parsley and paprika. Reheat before serving if necessary. Cut into slices.

Cubed Potatoes

Additions before cooking mean no fuss when serving.
These are good used in salads and cooked potato recipes, too.

For each serving
100g cubed raw potatoes
½ tsp butter or oil
2 tsp water
½ clove garlic, chopped
or 1-2 tsp chopped parsley
or spring onion

Scrub or peel potatoes. Cut in 15mm cubes, dropping these into a bowl of cold water, as prepared. Drain and put in oven bag or casserole. Add remaining ingredients, using oil if potatoes will be used for a salad. Cover. Estimate cooking time as for new potatoes. Shake container to coat evenly with thin film of butter and seasonings as soon as butter melts. Allow standing time of 3-4 minutes after cooking.

Globe Artichokes

Glove artichokes do not microwave as well as they cook conventionally.

Jerusalem Artichokes

Peel, slice thinly. Use general method, page 85, adding 1 tsp water per serving. 1-2 minutes per serving, depending on desired texture. Toss with chopped parsley and add pepper.
Use in stir-fries, or in julienne vegetable mixtures.

Asparagus

Choose good quality spears of even thickness. Fat spears cook better than very thin ones. Snap off bottom of stems. Peel bottom 5-6cm of stems with a potato peeler or sharp knife for best results and most even cooking.
Use an oven bag for a few servings, and a covered casserole for more. Melt 1-2 tsp butter per serving. Add prepared asparagus turning to coat. Add 1-2 tsp water per serving. Fold bag, excluding air. Cover casserole. Microwave on High (100% power).
10 medium stalks take about 2 minutes
500g asparagus takes 4-5 minutes.
Allow about 2 minutes standing time.
Do not overcook. Asparagus should be right green and slightly crunchy. Serve plain, or with hollandaise or cheese sauce.
Frozen asparagus. Cook 250g in 2 Tbsp water for 6-8 minutes.

Hollandaise Sauce

For 4 servings
100g butter
2 egg yolks
1 Tbsp lemon juice

Heat the butter in a 2 cup measuring cup, covered with a saucer to stop spatters, for 3 minutes on High (100% power). In a fairly small bowl with a rounded bottom beat the egg yolks with a whisk until well mixed. Add the hot butter to the egg yolks in a thin stream, whisking all the time. Do not add the butter sediment — ie stop after about ¾ of the butter is added.
The sauce should thicken as the hot butter is added. Whisk the lemon juice into the thickened sauce. This may thin the sauce considerably. If sauce needs further thickening microwave on defrost (30% power) for 1-1½ minutes, whisking after each 30 seconds. Stop as soon as sauce thickens round edge. Whisk to make sauce smooth. Serve sauce warm, not hot, warming carefully on defrost (30% power) for short intervals if necessary.
Variation: Replace lemon juice with orange juice if desired.

Green Beans

These take longer than you would expect. You may prefer to cook them conventionally.

Add ½ cup water to 500g sliced beans.

Cook at High (100% power) 8-15 minutes, depending on age. Stir at intervals.

Or use general method (page 85) for young, thinly sliced beans.

250g take 3-5 minutes
500g take 5-10 minutes

Add young beans to vegetable mixtures.

Frozen beans. Use general method, with butter and garlic.

250g need 6-8 minutes.

For toasted almonds toss ½ cup slivered almonds in 1 Tbsp melted butter. Cook on high (100% power) 2½-3 minutes until straw coloured. Sprinkle over cooked beans.

Dried Beans

See page 101.

Beetroot

Do not try cooking whole beets uncovered. Whole beets, covered with water, cook just as quickly by conventional methods. Raw cubes cook well.

Sweet sour cubed beetroot
500g beetroot, peeled and cubed
½ cup water
2 tsp cornflour
2 Tbsp sugar
½ tsp salt
2 Tbsp vinegar

Cut beetroot in 1cm cubes. Add water, cover, cook on High (100% power) 10 minutes. Mix remaining ingredients in order given. Add to beetroot. Cook 3 minutes longer, or until thickened.

Broccoli

Broccoli microwaves beautifully. Allow 125-150g per serving. Cut off heads, then peel stalks, pulling tough skin from base of stem towards tips. Cut peeled stalks into short lengths.

Add 2 tsp water per serving. Cook at High (100% power).
1 serving 1½ minutes
2 servings 2½ minutes
4 servings 4 minutes

Allow 2 minutes standing time. Toss with butter.

Or use general method, page 85. Unpeeled broccoli overcooks before stems become tender.

Frozen broccoli 250g 5-9 minutes, depending on size of frozen pieces. Serve with cheese sauce if desired.

Brussels Sprouts

Select small tight Brussel sprouts, allowing 75-100g per serving. Wash thoroughly. Remove outer leaves. Cut a deep cross in stem for even cooking.

Add 1-2 tsp water per serving. Microwave on High (100% power).
150-200g take about 3 minutes
300-400g take about 5 minutes.

Toss with butter and grated nutmeg.

Cabbage

Very good in microwave, keeping good colour and slight crunchiness. Add a little water for a softer texture. Allow 75-100g per serving. Slice thinly, removing thick ribs. Add 1 tsp water per serving if desired. Cook on High (100% power) 1-1½ minutes per serving. **or** cook using general method on page 85.
Include sliced cabbage in mixtures of vegetables.

Red Cabbage

For 4 servings
250g sliced red cabbage
1 onion, thinly sliced
1 apple, thinly sliced
2 Tbsp wine vinegar
2 tsp butter
½ tsp salt
1 Tbsp brown sugar

Combine first 5 ingredients in a covered casserole. Microwave on High (100% power) for 10-15 minutes, until tender. Stir in salt and brown sugar after 5 minute standing time.

Carrots

Young, early-season carrots microwave well.
Mid-season carrots cook well if they are cut into thin slices or thin strips. Old carrots are best avoided. If necessary, slice very thinly, or shred. Longer cooking shrivels old carrots, rather than making them more tender.
The cooking time varies with the maturity of the carrot and the size of the pieces. The amount of liquid needed increases with the maturity of the carrot. All pieces should be same size, thickness etc. Fruit juice, sugar, honey etc are best added after the carrots are cooked.

General method
Cut carrots into 5mm slices or long thin strips allowing about 75g per serving.
Add 1-4 tsp water per serving depending on age.
Add finely chopped herbs or poppy seeds or caraway seeds if desired.
Cover and cook 2-4 minutes per serving, depending on age.
Allow 2 minutes standing time.
Add butter, brown sugar or honey, orange juice and rind, nutmeg, or whatever flavourings you like. Add a little cornflour if desired. Reheat to glaze and thicken if desired.

Cauliflower

Cauliflower microwaves well.
Cut or break into evenly sized florets. Peel and chop stems as for broccoli if desired.
Allow 1-2 tsp water per 100g serving or add garlic and butter as in general method, page 85. Cook on High (100% power) allowing 1-2 minutes per serving.
Drain if necessary. Pile in serving dish. Sprinkle with grated cheese, paprika and parsley. If cheese does not melt straight away, reheat. Cauliflower cooks well in vegetable mixtures. For "stir-fries", cut florets into 5mm slices.

Celery

Celery microwaves well, keeping its bright colour.
Pull the strings from large stalks of celery before slicing them.
Allow 50-75g per serving.
It cooks evenly and looks attractive when sliced diagonally, or cut in julienne strips lengthwise.
Celery is a good addition to stir-fries, or to use in julienne strip mixtures (see page 95).

Braised Celery

For 4 servings
2-3 cups sliced celery
1 tsp powdered stock granules
½ tsp sugar
1 tsp cornflour
½ cup water
1 tsp butter
2 Tbsp chopped parsley

Combine all ingredients in a small covered casserole. Cook on High (100% power) for 5-6 minutes, stirring after 2 minutes.

Corn

Microwaved corn cooks fast and very easily in its husk.
Choose corn with green husks and plump kernels which puncture easily, and contain milky liquid.
To cook one, two or three cobs of corn. Lie cobs directly on floor or turntable of microwave oven, with spaces between two, or to form a triangle.
Microwave on High (100% power) allowing 3 minutes per cob.
Leave stand for 3-5 minutes before serving.
If you have more than three corn cobs, or if you have peeled corn cobs, put them in an oven bag with 1 Tbsp of water per corn cob.
Microwave 3-5 minutes per corn cob. Turn over and rearrange cobs several times during cooking.

Eggplant

Eggplant microwaves well. Eggplant which is to be puréed for other recipes may be baked whole. The baked flesh is pale green, rather than beige.
Puncture skin in several places. Bake at High (100% power), allowing about 6 minutes per 500g. Eggplant is cooked as soon as it feels soft all over. Allow 5 minutes standing time. Halve, and scoop out flesh, discarding skin.

Eggplant Dip

1 small eggplant (about 300g)
1 large clove garlic, chopped
¼ cup parsley
2 Tbsp lemon juice
2 Tbsp sesame paste (tahini)
salt and pepper

Cook whole eggplant as above, until just tender. Cube flesh. Mash with next four ingredients to desired consistency.
Season to taste with salt and cayenne pepper. Leave to stand for at least an hour, for flavours to blend. Serve with crackers, pita bread or melba toast.

Savoury Eggplant

1 eggplant (about 500g)
25g butter
2 cloves garlic, chopped
2 Tbsp chopped parsley

Just before cooking, cut unpeeled eggplant into 1cm cubes.
Heat butter and chopped garlic in a medium-sized casserole for 1 minute, then add the cubed eggplant and parsley. Cover and microwave on High (100% power)

for 5-8 minutes, or until tender, shaking or stirring twice.
Stand for 3 minutes then sprinkle with grated parmesan cheese, basil and oregano.

Kumara

Kumara microwave well, taking similar times to potatoes.

Baked Kumara

Scrub evenly shaped kumara well. Cut off any stringy ends. Prick in several places. Microwave on High (100% power), allowing 3 minutes per 100g, turning over after half the estimated cooking time. Cook until kumara gives when pressed. Leave to stand for 3-4 minutes.
Cut a cross in the top and press between cuts.
Serve with sour cream and chives, or with sour cream mixed with brown sugar in proportions to taste — e.g. 1 tsp brown sugar to 2 Tbsp sour cream.

Creamed Kumara

For 2 servings
300g kumara
2 Tbsp water
cream, milk and salt

Peel kumara and chop into 1cm lengths. Place in casserole. Add water, cover and cook on High (100% power) for 6 minutes or until just tender. Stand 3-5 minutes then mash, adding cream or sour cream, milk and salt to taste.

Leeks

Leeks take much longer in the

microwave oven than you might expect.
Cook conventionally, for preference. If microwaving use young, tender leeks, slice thinly, add liquid, and cover tightly during cooking.

Mushrooms

Mushrooms microwave very well, in a very short time.
Use firm-fleshed mushrooms for best results.
Follow general method on page 85, without adding any water. Cover loosely. Allow minimum cooking time.

Garlic Mushrooms

For 4 servings
400g mushrooms
2 cloves garlic, chopped
1 Tbsp butter
1 tsp light soya sauce
1 tsp cornflour
2 Tbsp chopped parsley or spring onion

Wipe mushrooms. Halve or slice if large. Chop garlic finely, and place with butter in a casserole dish just large enough to hold mushrooms. Heat at High (100% power) for 30 seconds or until butter has melted. Stir in soya sauce and cornflour, then toss mushrooms in this mixture, coating them evenly and lightly. Sprinkle with parsley or spring onion. Cover loosely and microwave for 3-4 minutes or until mushrooms have softened to the desired amount and are coated with lightly thickened sauce. Sprinkle with pepper.
Serve with steak etc, or serve on rice or toast.

Onions

Onions microwave well, whether finely chopped, sliced, halved or quartered, or cooked whole. They are often softened in butter or oil, to modify their flavour, before they are combined with other ingredients.

Caramelised Onion Rings

For 3-4 servings
1 Tbsp sugar
1 tsp water
25g butter
2-3 large onions
1 Tbsp water
½ tsp dark soya sauce
1 tsp wine vinegar

Combine sugar and water in a high-heat resistant dish. Microwave on High (100% power) until evenly golden brown. Add butter, sliced onions, water, dark soya sauce and vinegar.
Cover and cook for 3-6 minutes, or until onion is cooked to the desired degree. To thicken the sauce, uncover and cook about 1 minute more.
Spoon over sausages, steak etc.
Variation: Add 2 sliced apples and ½ tsp fresh sage to the onions after they have cooked for 3 minutes. Cook for about 5 minutes longer, until apples are tender.

Baked Onions

Peel small onions, cutting a thick slice from the top and bottom, so the centres do not pop out during cooking.
Put in a small covered casserole, allowing ½ tsp each of water and butter per serving.

Cook on High (100% power) allowing 1-2 minutes per onion.

Stuffed Onions

Slice tops and bottoms from large onions. Add ½ tsp each of butter and water per onion. Cover and cook on High (100% power) for 3 minutes per onion.
Lift out and chop the central portion of each onion. Mix with chopped parsley or other fresh herbs, fresh breadcrumbs, grated cheese, chopped nuts or minced meat etc. When required, cover and bake for about 3 minutes per onion.

Parsnips

The cooking time of parsnips varies. Check several times during cooking.
Peel and slice parsnips, allowing 75-100g per serving. Add 2tsp water per serving. Cover and cook on High (100% power), about 2 minutes per serving.

Glazed Parsnips

For 2 servings
1 medium parsnip (200g)
2 tsp butter
2 Tbsp brown sugar
1 Tbsp orange juice

Cut parsnip into pencil-thickness strips. Combine all ingredients in a small casserole. Cover and bake on High (100% power) for 6-8 minutes, or until barely tender. Leave to stand 2-3 minutes, turning to coat with glaze.

Parsnip-Carrot Mix

For 4 servings
2 cups grated carrot
2 cups grated parsnip
25g butter
¼ tsp salt
¼ cup water

Microwave all ingredients in a covered casserole for 8 minutes. Leave to stand for 3-4 minutes then mash, or purée in food processor. Add pepper to taste.

Peas

Frozen peas are at their best when microwaved, since none of their flavour is lost in cooking liquid.

For 1 serving
½ cup frozen peas
½ tsp butter
1 tsp water
1 sprig mint, optional
pinch sugar

Put everything together in a small casserole, oven bag or a double layered packet of greaseproof paper.
Cook on High (100% power) for 1-1½ minutes.
For larger quantities allow 1-2 minutes per ½ cup serving, and stir several times during cooking.

Savoury Peas

For 4 servings
1 Tbsp butter
½ cup thinly sliced celery
1 Tbsp flour
2 Tbsp water
½ cup chopped spring onions
2 cups frozen peas
¼ tsp salt
½ tsp sugar

In medium-sized covered casserole microwave butter and celery on High (100% power) for 2 minutes. Stir in remaining ingredients and mix well. Cook for about 4 minutes,

or until sauce thickens, stirring aftrer 2 minutes.

Peppers

Plump, crisp red, green and yellow peppers microwave well, alone, in mixtures of julienne strips or in stir-fried mixtures.
Cook to desired degree of tenderness. Red and yellow peppers keep their colour. Green peppers turn olive green with prolonged cooking.

Sesame Peppers

2-4 servings
1 Tbsp corn or soya soil
1 clove garlic, chopped
1/2 tsp sesame oil
1/2 tsp light soya sauce
1 green pepper, sliced
1 red pepper, sliced
1/4 tsp cornflour (optional)
pinch sugar
1 Tbsp toasted sesame seeds

Combine first six ingredients in a medium-sized covered casserole. Microwave on High (100% power) for 3-4 minutes, until tender-crisp. Thicken liquid with cornflour if desired, add sugar and cook 1 minute longer.
Sprinkle with sesame seeds before serving with steak, chops etc.

Pumpkin

This is easy and good in the microwave.
Whole — When you have a whole pumpkin and want purée for pies and soup, put it in the oven just as it is and microwave on High (100% power) turning over, every now and then, until the flesh "gives" all over, when pressed. A 1½kg

pumpkin will take 15-20 minutes. Halve, discard seeds, then scoop out and sieve the flesh to use as you like.
Wedges — Remove seeds from wedge, place in an unsealed oven bag, cook until it feels tender through the bag 5-7 minutes per 500g.

Creamy Pumpkin Cubes

400g cubed pumpkin
2 tsp flour
1 garlic clove, chopped
1/2 tsp curry powder (optional)
1/4 tsp salt
1/4 cup cream, creamy milk,
  or coconut cream
chopped spring onion

Cut pumpkin in 1cm cubes. Toss to coat with flour.
Add remaining ingredients except spring onion. Cover and cook at High (100% power) until pumpkin is tender, stirring several times, for 5-8 minutes.
Variations: Leave out curry powder. Sprinkle cooked pumpkin with cinnamon sugar.

Golden Casserole

Serves 8
1 cup dried haricot beans or
  chickpeas
1.5kg pumpkin
2 onions, chopped
2 garlic cloves, chopped
50g butter
2 cups grated cheese
tabasco sauce
salt and pepper

Cook beans (see page 101).
Cook pumpkin (see above).
Chop onions and garlic. Cook, with

butter in a large covered casserole, at High (100% power) for 4 minutes. Add pumpkin, mix in with fork without mashing smooth. Stir in drained beans or chickpeas, grated cheese and tabasco. Taste and season to taste with pepper and salt. Reheat until centre bottom is hot.
Sprinkle with grated cheese, paprika and parsley.

Silverbeet

Cook young silverbeet as spinach, with steams sliced very thinly.

Spinach

Easy and good!
Wash spinach well, place in oven bag or large casserole, removing stems. Secure bag loosely with rubber band or cover casserole. Microwave on High (100% power) until spinach is cooked, 1-2 minutes per serving. Squeeze bag, drain off juice, chop spinach. Use cooked spinach as desired.
or for each serving heat 1 tsp butter and 1 tsp flour add 1½ Tbsp cream and 1/4 tsp powdered chicken stock. Stir in drained spinach and reheat until bubbling.

Swede

There is little advantage in microwaving swede, since it cooks conventionally in the same time. For 4 servings cube 250g peeled swede. Add 1 Tbsp bacon fat or butter and 1 Tbsp each water and parsley. Cover and cook until tender, 6-8 minutes. Serve as is, or mash.
Use suede in julienne vegetable mixtures.

Tomatoes

Tomatoes cook very quickly and well. Always pierce skins of whole tomatoes by cutting a cross in the rounded end. Halve or cut in thick slices if preferred. Cooking times vary with temperature, ripeness and size of tomatoes.

Baked Tomato Halves

4 servings
500g fairly large, red tomatoes
2 tsp butter
sugar
salt
basil, thyme, spring onions or parsley

Halve tomatoes. Place close together, cut side up, in shallow baking dish.
Dot surface with butter. Sprinkle with sugar, salt and herbs.
Bake uncovered, on High (100% power) for 2-4 minutes, until tomatoes are just soft.

Sliced Tomatoes

Arrange thickly sliced tomatoes on a buttered dish. Sprinkle with salt, sugar, pepper, chopped spring onions or other herbs. Bake until hot but not too soft, allowing about 30 seconds per tomato. Watch carefully to prevent overcooking.
Variation: Add herbed crumbs (below)

Stuffed Tomatoes

4 large tomatoes
2 spring onions, chopped
2-4 mushrooms, chopped
2 tsp butter
¼ cup herbed crumbs
salt, pepper, sugar

fresh herbs, chopped

Cut tops off tomatoes or halve tomatoes and scoop out pulp. Cook onions, mushrooms and butter on High (100% power) in a small covered container for 2 minutes. Add tomato pulp, herbed crumbs and more fresh herbs if desired. Taste and adjust seasoning.
Pile filling into or onto tomatoes. Cover lightly in a shallow dish. Bake until tomatoes have heated through.

Herbed Crumbs
25g butter
1½ cups fresh breadcrumbs
1 Tbsp chopped parsley
2 tsp chopped basil (optional)
1 Tbsp parmesan cheese (optional)

Melt butter in shallow casserole. Stir in crumbs and herbs and cheese, if used. Microwave about 2 minutes, until golden brown.

Tomato Juice

When tomatoes are plentiful, put about 1kg of whole, ripe, red, fleshy tomatoes in a large, covered casserole dish with a few sprigs of parsley, thyme, basil etc, a generous grinding of fresh pepper, 1 tsp sugar and ½ tsp salt. Cover. Microwave on High (100% power) until tomatoes are soft, 6-8 minutes. Purée in food processor then shake through sieve. Chill in refrigerator, adjusting seasoning carefully with worcestershire sauce, tabasco sauce, wine vinegar, salt and more sugar if desired.
Serve over ice.
Vary flavourings to suit your taste.

Yams

Small pink yams may be microwaved according to the general vegetable method on page 85.
Slice yams diagonally, or halve lengthways. Allow about 4 minutes per 100g serving.

Sweet Sour Yams

For 2 servings
200-250g scrubbed yams
1 Tbsp butter
1 Tbsp brown sugar
1 Tbsp wine vinegar
1 tsp cornflour
2 Tbsp water

Slice yams crosswise into 1cm slices. Heat butter, brown sugar and wine vinegar in a medium-sized casserole dish on High (100% power) for 2 minutes. Sprinkle cornflour over sliced yams. Add these, with water, to sugar mixture. Cover and cook for 5 minutes, or to desired tenderness.
Season to taste with salt and pepper. Add a little extra water if sauce not smooth when yams are cooked. Stir to coat with sauce.

Zucchini

Fresh, plump zucchini microwave well, alone or with other vegetables.
Use the same method for green zucchini, yellow zucchini and scallopini.
Allow about 75g per serving. Use general method on page 85, adding 1 tsp water per serving.
Use zucchini in vegetable mixtures, julienne strips etc.

Herbed Zucchini in Cream

For 3-4 servings
200-300g zucchini, sliced
2 tsp butter

1 clove garlic, chopped
½ tsp chopped rosemary
¼ cup cream

Combine all ingredients in a shallow covered caserole. Microwave at High (100% power) for 2-3 minutes, until zucchini are tender crisp, shaking casserole to mix after 1½ minutes. Uncover and cook 2 minutes longer, until cream sauce thickens. Stir to coat zucchini and serve immediately.

Julienne Vegetable Strips

Long thin strips of vegetables look attractive and cook quickly together, in the microwave oven. The strips should be thicker than matches but thinner than pencils. Cut vegetables with longer cooking times (like carrots) into the thinnest strips.

For 2 servings
50g carrots
50g zucchini
50g celery
1 tsp butter
2 Tbsp water
1 finely chopped garlic
  clove (optional)
1-4 tsp chopped fresh herbs

Cut carrots, zucchini and celery into thin strips, making the carrot strips the thinnest, if carrots are fairly mature.
Put vegetable strips with butter, water and garlic into a small microwave casserole.
Cover and cook on High (100% power) for 3-4 minutes, until barely tender, shaking vegetables to coat with butter after 2 minutes. Leave to stand for 2 minutes, then sprinkle with finely chopped parsley or other fresh herbs.

Other suitable vegetables to replace or add to the above vegetables include white turnips, swede, long white radish, green peppers, red peppers, yellow peppers, yellow zucchini.

Stir-fried Vegetables

For 4 servings
500g sliced quick cooking
  vegetables
1-2 garlic cloves, chopped
2 Tbsp oil
1 tsp cornflour
½ tsp chicken stock powder
2 tsp brown sugar
1 Tbsp dry sherry
1 tsp light soya sauce

Cut vegetables into slices so that they will cook in the same time. Slice slower-cooking vegetables thinly, and quick-cooking vegetables in thicker slices. Heat chopped garlic and oil in casserole dish large enough to hold vegetables. Microwave on High (100% power) for 2 minutes, then add vegetables and toss to coat with oil.
Cover and cook for 3-5 minutes, shaking or stirring after 2 minutes, until tender crisp. Mix remaining ingredients to a smooth paste, stir into vegetables and cook 1 minute longer. Stir to coat. Vegetables should be lightly coated with glaze. Serve as soon as possible.

Savoury Sauces

Sauces are smoother, creamier and quicker and easier when made in a microwave oven.
These sauces make good accompaniments for many vegetables. If you make the sauce before you cook the vegetable, you can pour the cooked sauce over the

vegetable, sprinkle it with chopped parsley etc. and reheat both when it suits you.

White Sauce

2-3 Tbsp butter
2-3 Tbsp flour
1 cup milk
¼ tsp salt

Melt butter in a 2 cup measure at High (100% power) for 30-40 seconds.
Stir in flour and heat until mixture bubbles. Remove from oven before mixture browns. Stir in the milk and microwave until sauce bubbles around the edge of the measuring cup.
Stir thoroughly and heat again. Total cooking time after milk is added should be about 3 minutes. Remove from oven and stir well. Season carefully, adding no more salt than necessary, and adding pepper to taste.
Variations: Use the larger quantities of butter and flour for a thicker sauce. Replace all or half the milk with vegetable or meat stock. Stir in a little cream at the end.

Parsley Sauce
Stir ¼ cup finely chopped parsley into the sauce after its final cooking.

Cheese Sauce
Stir ½-1 cup grated tasty cheese into the sauce after its final cooking, before adding salt. Reheat sauce briefly to melt cheese if necessary, without letting sauce boil again.

Note: If not using sauces immediately, cover surface with plastic film to prevent a skin forming or run a little extra liquid over the surface of the finished sauce.

95

Grains, Pulses & Pasta

Grain, Pulses & Pasta

Once I started cooking rice in my microwave oven, I stopped cooking it any other way! Microwaved rice does not cook dramatically quickly, because it needs time to soak up the liquid, but it has other important advantages.

It needs no attention while it cooks or after cooking. It doesn't burn on the bottom or need draining afterwards.

It is easy to reheat, without needing additions — in fact it may be cooked, served, refrigerated and reheated in the same dish. It's flavour is excellent, and the yield large. I hope you will be now tempted to microwave other grains too!

Porridge making is revolutionised by microwaving. Each person can make the porridge he likes best, and there is no messy pot to wash. If you prefer muesli to porridge, you will find it easy to microwave, too.

Pulses — dried peas, beans and lentils microwave well, but not particularly fast. The cooking time is halved if they are soaked first. Like rice, they need no watching or stirring, and of course they stop cooking at a set time, whether you are there or not.

Most cooks prefer to microwave the sauces that they serve with spaghetti, noodles etc. and boil the pasta conventionally. I do, too, but find that some pasta mixtures microwave well, and reheat well, too.

Rice

Microwaved rice is easy and trouble free. Although you can cook any type of rice in your microwave oven, you will probably find, as I do, that you get best results when you use long grain rice which has been heat-treated, and which is a yellowish colour when you buy it. This rice usually costs a little more, but a cup of this rice produces a greater volume of cooked rice, with grains that separate well, without stickiness, so I consider it worthwhile.

Sushi

For this modified sushi recipe, short grain rice is cooked in plain water until it has absorbed all its liquid. It is then flavoured with a sweetened vinegar mixture. The sticky, seasoned sushi rice may then be used in different ways.

1 cup short grain rice
2 cups water
2 Tbsp dry sherry
2 Tbsp wine vinegar
2 Tbsp sugar
1 tsp salt

Cook the rice and water in a 2 litre covered casserole on High (100% power) for 10 minutes. Stir in the remaining ingredients and heat 2 minutes longer. Leave until warm, before shaping.
(a) Squeeze small handfuls of sushi rice, to make egg shaped cakes. Cover each of these with a thin slice of smoked salmon or any other firm fresh fish, which has been dipped in a mixture of:

2 Tbsp water
1 Tbsp wine vinegar
1 tsp sugar
½ tsp salt

(b) Make flattened round cakes. Top with oysters which have been dipped in the sauce above.
(c) Lightly toast a sheet of thin dried seaweed (from a store which supplies Japanese food).
Place on a sheet of plastic, then spread evenly with some of the sushi rice. Top with strips of thin omelette, strips of crisp carrot, cucumber or celery, and strips of smoked salmon. Roll like a sponge roll. Wrap in plastic. When firm, cut in 1-2cm thick slices, and serve as appetisers.

Spiced Rice

3-4 servings
1 cup long-grain rice (preferably heat treated)
1 tsp salt
1 cinnamon stick
6 cloves
3-4 drops hot pepper sauce
2 cups hot water
2 chopped garlic cloves
3 Tbsp butter
3-4 eggs
3 Tbsp water

Measure first five ingredients into a 2 litre casserole. Add hot water and half the garlic, cover and microwave on High (100% power) for 12 minutes. Leave to stand without uncovering, while you make savoury scrambled eggs in medium-sized bowl. Heat remaining garlic and butter for 1½ minutes. Add eggs and water, beat with a fork until mixed. Stir into garlic butter. Microwave, stirring after 1 minute until egg increases in volume. Without allowing standing time, stir egg through rice from which cloves and cinnamon have been removed.

Coconut Rice

This rice has an interesting coconut flavour and is especially good with curries. Try leftovers, reheated with sultanas, and served with cinnamon sugar, as a breakfast cereal!

4 servings:
1 cup long grain rice
  (preferably heat treated)
½ tsp salt
1¾ cups hot water
1 cup coconut cream

Measure rice, salt and hot water into a 2 litre casserole. Cover and cook on High (100% power) for 10 minutes. Uncover, add coconut cream, and cook 5 minutes longer, covered loosely with a paper towel or greaseproof paper. Leave to stand for 5-10 minutes before serving.
Variation: Add a finely chopped garlic clove, and ½ tsp turmeric to the uncooked rice. Proceed as above.

Basic Rice

4 servings

1 cup long grain rice
  (preferably heat treated)
2-3tsp butter or oil
½ tsp salt or 1 tsp powdered
  stock granules
2¼ cups very hot water

Put rice in a fairly deep, 2 litre casserole dish, since it boils up during cooking. Add the butter or oil, the salt or powdered stock (any suitable flavour) then pour in the hot water. Stir, cover and cook on High (100% power) for 12 minutes. Stand, for 5-8 minutes, toss with a fork.

To prepare ahead, cook as above, then reheat for about 3 minutes. For 2 cups rice double everything, use boiling water, and cook 20 minutes. Stand 10 minutes.

Variation:
If you have trouble with rice boiling over, cook for longer at low power. Use boiling water, then cook at defrost (30% power) for 20 minutes.

Savoury Rice

4 servings

25g butter or oil
1 onion, finely chopped
1-2 garlic cloves, chopped
¼-½ cup finely chopped celery
  or red or green pepper
1 cup long grain rice
2 cups very hot water
½ tsp salt
2-4 Tbsp chopped parsley

Heat butter or oil and vegetables in a covered 2 litre microwave casserole dish on High (100% power) for 3 minutes, stirring after 1 minute.

Add the rice, stir well and cook for 2 minutes longer.

Add the hot water and salt, cover, and cook for 12 minutes.

Leave to stand for 5 minutes, then stir in the chopped parsley and serve.

Savoury Brown Rice

Follow recipe for Savoury Rice using brown rice, and 2½ cups boiling water. After adding water cover and cook for 20 minutes.

Kibbled Rye

Cook kibbled rye, according to the instructions given for basic Brown Rice or Savoury Brown Rice. It has a darker colour, but no more flavour than kibbled wheat.

Cooked without butter or oil, it makes a type of porridge, and may be used in mixed-grain porridge.

Kibbled Wheat

Kibbled wheat is wheat which has been chopped into pieces, sometimes quite large, and sometimes small. These pieces unlike bulgar (or burghul) have not been pre-cooked and redried. Kibbled wheat microwaves very well, and has a more interesting flavour than brown rice. It may be used just as rice is, and is especially good when served with lamb. Very finely chopped kibbled wheat cooks more quickly than coarsely chopped kibbled wheat does.

To microwave kibbled wheat follow the instructions for cooking rice. Leftover, cold savoury kibbled wheat makes the basis of a good salad. Add well-seasoned oil and vinegar dressing, fresh herbs and crunchy salad vegetables to taste. Cooked without oil or butter, kibbled wheat is more sticky, and is sometimes included in mixed grain porridges. Very finely chopped kibbled wheat is best for this.

Brown Rice

Brown, unpolished rice takes 45-50 minutes to cook when simmered on the stove-top, but microwaves in a much shorter time. It has more flavour, more B vitamins, and a chewier texture than white rice. Brown rice grains, short or long, tend to stay separate, during and after cooking.

Basic Brown Rice:
4 servings
1 cup brown rice
1 Tbsp butter or oil
½ tsp salt
2½ cups boiling water

Combine all ingredients, in the order given, in a 2 litre covered casserole dish.

Microwave on high (100% power) for 20 minutes, then leave to stand for 10 minutes before uncovering and forking over lightly.

Hot Breakfast Cereals

If you like porridge but hate soaking and washing a porridge pot, you'll find that your worries are over with your porridge microwaved.

Make and serve the porridge in the same bowl. Choose a bowl that will be only half filled by the quantity of cereal you mix. This leaves room for bubbling. Choose a fairly deep bowl rather than a wide shallow one.

Unless you have a large family, all wanting their cereal at the same time, make the porridge in separate plates. You can measure out the cereal, water and salt into each plate and leave each family member to cook their own. Different types of porridge require slightly different amounts of liquid. Start with these proportions and change them until you have your porridge exactly the way you like it.

Plain Porridge

¼ cup rolled oats
(or other uncooked breakfast cereal)
½ cup hot tap water
⅛ tsp salt

Put the cereal in the plate, add the hot water (for speed) and the salt. Microwave on High (100% power) for 1 minute, then stir. Microwave 1-1½ minutes longer, until the porridge has changed colour in the middle of the plate. Stir again, and

stand for 1 minute before serving. It is a good idea to stir with a rubber scraper. You can run it around the plate during the second stirring, cleaning the edge so it doesn't look as if the porridge was cooked in the plate.

Note: This recipe makes a fairly small serving. Increase quantities, using the same proportions and cook for a little longer.

Whole-Grain Oat Porridge

Porridge made from flaked, whole grain oats has a coarser texture than porridge made from plain rolled oats. Use the same proportions but cook for ½-1 minute longer, depending on the texture you like.

Mixed Grain Porridge

You can make interesting breakfast cereal mixtures by combining different grains.

I keep jars of kibbled wheat, kibbled rye, rolled oats, wholegrain oats, toasted sesame seeds, wheat bran, oat bran and wheatgerm at the back of my kitchen bench. For each serving of porridge I select a tablespoon of each of four of these.

This is ¼ cup altogether. I pour ½ cup hot tap water over these, and add ⅛ teaspoon salt.

Microwave cereal in the plate for 1 minute on high (100% power), stir

and microwave again for 2 minutes. Stir again, and leave to stand for 2 minutes.

For a larger serving, use 6 tablespoons of the above, and add ¾ cup water and a little extra salt.

Serving Cooked Cereals

These cereals have such a good flavour that you may find you like them best without any added sweetener.

If not, sweeten them with white or brown sugar, plain, dark or fruit flavoured honey or golden syrup. Vary the liquid you pour onto porridge. Use milk, plain or flavoured yoghurt, evaporated milk, condensed milk, cream or sour cream.

Muesli

This is, without a doubt, the easiest muesli I make!

½ cup honey
¼ cup brown sugar
¼ cup oil
1 tsp cinnamon
1 tsp vanilla
½ tsp salt
3 cups whole grain oats
½ cup oat bran
½ cup coconut
½ cup wheatgerm
½ cup chopped nuts
½ cup dried fruit

Mix the first six ingredients in a bowl. Heat at High (100%) power until mixture bubbles, about two minutes. Meantime, combine remaining ingredients except dried fruit in a large, wide shallow

microwave dish. Stir in the hot mixture.

Cook, stirring every minute after four minutes, until mixture turns golden brown and starts to firm up, from 6-10 minutes. Cool. Break up if necessary. Store in airtight jars when cold.

Dried Beans

1 cup dried haricot beans
4 cups boiling water

Pour boiling water over beans in a large bowl or casserole and leave to stand for an hour, if possible. If cooking immediately, microwave at Defrost (30% power) for 1-1½ hours, using the shorter time if beans are to be combined with other ingredients and recooked. For bean salads etc, check to see if beans are very tender after 1¼ hours.
If leaving beans to stand before cooking, bring them to the boil on High (100% power) for about 10 minutes, then cook at Defrost (30% power) for 30-45 minutes.

Dried Peas

Use method similar to that for dried beans. Smaller or split peas will cook in a shorter time, and do not need soaking.

Brown Lentils

1 cup brown lentils
3 cups boiling water

Pour boiling water over lentils and leave to stand until ready to cook. Use method as for dried beans but reduce cooking times.
Soaked lentils will cook to barely tender stage in as little as 10 minutes.
Unsoaked lentils take about 30 minutes to reach this stage. Allow about 10 minutes longer to reach very soft stage.

Adding Flavourings: Bayleaves or other herbs, chopped onion, garlic, carrots and celery etc may be added during initial or later cooking, for extra flavour. Do not add salt, sugar etc until pulses are tender, since they slow down the cooking.

Pasta

When you are cooking spaghetti or noodles plainly, and intend to drain them, butter them lightly and serve them with a sauce, you are best to cook them conventionally, while you make the sauce (or reheat it) in your microwave oven.
When you are cooking pasta which is to be served in a thickened sauce, you may find that the microwave oven simplifies your task. See the recipe for Macaroni Cheese on page 25. You can cook meat and macaroni mixtures quite successfully, too.
Lasagne and other layered mince and pasta recipes microwave well. I cook my favourite, easy lasagne recipes very successfully, starting with raw pasta. See page 62.
I find the microwave oven very useful for reheating drained, cooked pasta in creamy sauces.

Creamy Noodles

2-3 servings
2 cups cooked noodles
about ¼ cup sour cream
about ¼ cup milk, or more sour cream
½ tsp onion, celery or garlic salt or stock granules
¼ cup chopped parsley or spring onion
1-3 tsp chopped fresh herbs

Put the cooked noodles in an unpunctured oven bag or casserole dish.
Add the liquid, seasoning, and herbs. If the noodles can be separated, mix together lightly, otherwise fasten bag with a rubber band, leaving a finger-sized hole, or cover casserole and heat for 3-4 minutes on High (100% power) stirring once, when noodles are hot enough to be separated. When noodles are hot right through, shake in bag (with air in the bag) or stir gently.
Adjust seasoning and quantity of liquid if necessary.
Cream will be absorbed if noodles are left to stand.
Variations. Replace herbs with small amounts of poppy seeds or caraway seeds, or finely chopped nuts or toasted sunflower seeds. Replace sour cream and milk with unsweetened yoghurt.

Desserts

Desserts

A microwave oven will encourage you to make desserts frequently! You will find it a wonderful help, whether you want filling, warming puddings for a large and hungry family or want something to end a special dinner for one or two.
Sauces, custards and puddings turn out velvety and smooth.
Steamed puddings cook in a few minutes instead of hours.
Baked apples and crumbles are child's play.
You will have to restructure your pie making but the new techniques give good results in a short time. The selection of desserts included here should prove interesting to you to make, as well as delicious. Using these recipes as a guide, you should be able to modify many of your own family favourites.

Baked Apples

I bake apples on individual serving dishes.

For 1 baked apple:
1 large apple
1 tsp rolled oats
2 tsp brown sugar
2 dates, chopped
1 tsp butter
1/4 tsp cinnamon

Core the apple by cutting a cone shape out of the top and then removing the lower part of the core with an apple corer. You should then have a large cavity to fill with stuffing. Chop the removed apple flesh with rolled oats, brown sugar and dates (or other dried fruit or nuts). Pile back into apple. Top with butter and sprinkle with cinnamon. Cover with cling wrap, leaving a vent for steam. Microwave on High (100% power) for 2-3 minutes, then test with a skewer. Continue cooking until flesh is barely tender. Do not overcook because apple will cook a little more as it stands. Serve hot, warm, cold, or reheated, with cream, custard or ice cream. (If apple overcooks and filling spills out during cooking, pile it back before serving.) When several apples are arranged in a circle in a large covered dish, they may need to be rotated so they cook evenly.

Baked Apple Sauce

When you have a lot of apples, make this simple apple sauce. Put the uncored whole apples in a suitable large casserole dish. Cover and microwave on High (100% power), allowing 2-4 minutes for each apple, depending on variety. When apples are soft and cool enough to handle, push or bang them through a sieve, discarding skin and cores. Add a little sugar to the puréed mixture.
Apple Fool: Fold 1 cup whipped cream into 2 cups of cold, sweetened apple puree.

Caramel Bananas

For 4 servings:
3 or 4 medium firm bananas
2 Tbsp butter
1/4 cup packed brown sugar
1/2 tsp cinnamon
2 Tbsp cream
1/4 tsp rum essence or 2 Tbsp rum
1/4 cup chopped walnuts

Slice bananas in half, both lengthwise and crosswise. Place butter in a casserole and microwave on High (100% power) for 30 seconds or until melted. Add the sugar, spice and cream, stir and heat for 1½-2 minutes, or until slightly thickened. Stir in rum or essence. Add the bananas, turning each to coat with sauce. Microwave again for 30 seconds and serve sprinkled with nuts.

Stewed Fruit

Fruit stews well, with very good flavour and texture.
For preference, use a flat-bottomed round casserole dish with a lid. For small quantities, stew fruit in a ring pan. This gives even results.
You will find that soft fruits with a high water content, will cook well with no added water. Add sugar to taste afterwards, stirring gently until it dissolves. Or, cook a small amount of syrup first, then cook the fruit in this until it is tender.
If you want fruit to keep its shape, stew it at a lower power level for a longer time (see the apricots and rhubarb photographed).
For a thickened fruit mixture, mix fruit, sugar and thickening together (e.g. fruit pie filling) or prepare the sweetened, thickened sauce, then cook the fruit in it as in Rhubarb Sago (page 105).

Sour Cream Sauce

½ cup brown sugar
½ cup créme frâiche or sour cream
½ tsp vanilla

In a small jug or bowl mix the sugar, créme frâiche and vanilla. Microwave on High (100% power) for 30-60 seconds, or until sugar melts. Do not boil. Stir until smooth and cool to room temperature. Serve with ice cream, raw or cooked fruit, plain puddings, etc. **Sour Cream Coffee Sauce**: Add 1 tsp instant coffee mixed with 1 tsp water. Serve with ice-cream and bananas.

Orange Sauce

½ cup sugar
1 Tbsp cornflour or custard powder
50g butter
1 orange, grated rind and juice
juice of ½ lemon
½ cup water

Stir together sugar and custard powder in a bowl or 2-cup measure. Add remaining ingredients. Microwave on High (100% power) for 5-6 minutes, stirring every minute after 3 minutes. Serve warm on ice cream, with or without sliced bananas.
Variation: Replace orange with a tangelo.

Raspberry Sauce

½ cup sugar
1 Tbsp custard powder
½ cup water or white wine
2 cups frozen raspberries
2-3 Tbsp rum or brandy (optional)

In a small bowl or jug microwave the sugar, custard powder and liquid on High (100/% power) until bubbling. Stir, then boil for 1-2 minutes. Stir in the thawed raspberries, mashing if desired. Add flavouring, if used. Serve warm or cold, with ice cream, cream or plain pudding or cake.

Peanut Chocolate Sauce

¾ cup (½ packet) chocolate morsels
¼ cup peanut butter
¼ cup milk

In a small bowl or jug microwave all of the ingredients on Medium (50% power) for 2 minutes. Stir until smooth. Thin with extra milk. The sauce will thicken on cooling. Reheat before use. Extra milk may be needed to thin the sauce after reheating it. Serve over ice cream, with or without bananas. Note: Use smooth or crunchy peanut butter.

Lemon Sauce

1½ Tbsp custard powder or cornflour
2 Tbsp sugar
1 Tbsp golden syrup
¾ cup water
1 lemon, grated rind and juice
1 Tbsp butter

Stir dry ingredients together in a 2-cup measuring jug or bowl. Add a rounded household spoon of syrup, then remaining ingredients. Microwave on High (100% power) for 5 minutes, stirring every minute after 3 minutes. Serve warm with ice cream, steamed pudding or gingerbread.

Caramel Nut Sauce

½ cup brown sugar
75g butter, cubed
2 Tbsp water
¼ cup chopped walnuts
½ tsp vanilla or rum flavouring

Combine the sugar, butter and water in a 2-cup glass measuring cup. Microwave on High (100% power) for 4 minutes, stirring after 2 minutes. (Sauce should bubble rapidly for 1½ minutes.) Stir in chopped walnuts and vanilla or rum flavouring. Serve warm, reheating if necessary. Serve with ice cream, and/or peaches or with plain cake.

Sago or Tapioca Cream

For 4 servings:
1/4 cup sago or quick-cooking
    tapioca
2 cups milk
1/4 tsp vanilla
1/8 tsp salt
1/4 cup sugar
1 egg, separated

Mix the sago and milk in a large bowl or casserole. Cook uncovered on High (100% power) for 10-12 minutes, stirring every 2-3 minutes until sago is tender. (Note: bowl must be large and uncovered or the mixture will boil over.) Stir in vanilla, salt, 3 Tbsp of the sugar, and the egg yolk, putting aside the egg white in another bowl. Microwave sago mixture for 3 minutes, stirring each minute, until bubbling. Beat egg white until foamy. Add remaining Tbsp of sugar. Beat until peaks turn over. Fold the beaten egg white into the hot sago and serve warm, plain or layered with whipped cream, mashed kiwifruit, strawberries, etc.

Rhubarb Sago

For 4 servings:
1/4 cup sago
1 1/2 cups hot tap water
500g (4 cups) chopped rhubarb
1/2 cup sugar

Put the sago and hot tap water into a covered dish about 23cm in diameter. Cover and microwave on High (100% power) for 3-4 minutes until the sago mixture has thickened and nearly all the grains of sago have gone clear. Stir in the rhubarb, chopped into short (1cm) lengths, and the sugar. Cover again and microwave for 3 minutes, then stir well. Microwave for 3-4 minutes longer until all rhubarb pieces are hot. Leave to stand for 5 minutes — rhubarb should finish cooking in this time.

Fruit Salad Sago

For 4 servings:
1/4 cup sago
1 cup water
1 cup fruit juice, made up with a
little water or sherry if necessary
1/2 cup sugar
1 cup drained pineapple pieces
1 cup drained peach slices
2 passionfruit (optional)
1-2 bananas, sliced

In a medium sized bowl, add the water to the sago and leave to stand 15 minutes. Microwave on High (100% power) for 3 minutes. Add the other liquid, stir and cook 5 minutes longer. Add the fruit and allow to stand for 10-15 minutes, then spoon into individual serving dishes. Serve with cream. This pudding is best served warm, within 2 hours. Longer standing makes it rather tough, and spoils the flavour.

Variation: Replace sago with quick cooking tapioca.

Tamarillo Cream

For 4 servings:

4 tamarillos, halved
1/2 cup brown sugar
1/4 cup sugar
2 tsp gelatine
1 cup cream
1/2 tsp vanilla

Cut the stem end off each unpeeled tamarillo. Cut each lengthwise. Place halves in a flat-bottomed casserole, cut surface down. Cover and microwave on High (100% power) for 2-4 minutes or until skins lift. Remove skins. Sprinkle the sugars over the tamarillos. Purée with potato masher. Heat briefly until sugar dissolves, if necessary. Cool. Sprinkle with gelatine, leave 2-3 minutes, then stir. Microwave for 1 minute, stirring until gelatine melts. Cool over ice and water until cold and beginning to thicken. In another bowl beat the cream and vanilla until thick. Fold the cream into the tamarillos. Pile into stemmed glasses or individual dessert dishes and serve. Garnish with slices of fresh tamarillo.
Variations: (a) Stir in 2 cups plain yoghurt instead of cream. (b) Place more cold, cooked tamarillos in serving dishes, underneath the tamarillo cream.

Microwaving Custard

Stirred microwaved custard doesn't cook any more quickly than custard cooked in a pot, but you benefit in other ways.

1. You won't have a sticky-bottomed pot to clean.
2. You set the cooking time, so your custard will stop cooking even if you get called away.
3. You don't have to stir the custard all the time.
4. Microwaved custards are as smooth as velvet!

Simon's Custard

For twenty years the mothers of young children have told me how useful they have found this recipe.

1-1½ Tbsp cornflour
2 tsp white or brown sugar
1½ cups milk
2 egg yolks
1-2 tsp butter

Mix the cornflour and sugar together in a 1 litre measuring bowl/cup. Add enough milk to blend them to a smooth paste, then break in the egg yolks. Mix well. Add the rest of the milk, then the pieces of butter. Microwave on High (100% power) for 5-6 minutes, stirring after 3,4 and 5 minutes.
When it is cooked, the whole surface of the custard should have bubbled up. Take it out of the oven and stir well.
Note: Use the smaller quantity of cornflour if you want a custard thin enough to pour.

Variations:
(a) Replace the cornflour with vanilla custard powder.
(b) Use one whole egg instead of two egg yolks.

Chocolate Pudding

¼ cup cocoa
¼ cup sugar
3 Tbsp cornflour or custard powder
2 cups milk
½ tsp vanilla
1 Tbsp butter
1 egg

Stir together the cocoa, sugar and cornflour. Using a whisk, gradually stir in the milk. Add vanilla. Microwave on High (100% power) for 6 minutes stirring after 3, 4, and 5 minutes. After whole surface of custard has bubbled, add butter and stir until it is melted. Break egg on top of pudding, then quickly whisk it into mixture. Microwave 1 minute or until custard bubbles again. Beat thoroughly with a whisk. Cover surface with cling wrap to prevent skin forming.

Caramel Custard

Serve with peaches, or over sherry-sprinkled sponge to make trifle.

¼ cup brown sugar
¼ cup custard powder
2 cups milk
1 tsp vanilla
2 Tbsp butter

Mix the brown sugar and custard powder thoroughly in a fairly large bowl. Stir in milk and vanilla. Add butter and microwave on High (100% power) for 6 minutes, stirring after 3, 4 and 5 minutes.

Custard should bubble over whole surface. Cover. Serve warm or at room temperature.
Note: For Banana Custard, stir in 1-2 thinly sliced ripe bananas when custard is bath temperature. Add an egg or egg yolk with the milk, if desired.

"Baked" Custard

For successful custards preheat the milk, use individual dishes and low power levels.

For 4 servings:
2 cups milk
¼ cup sugar
pinch salt
3 eggs, beaten
1 tsp vanilla
ground nutmeg

Microwave milk on High (100% power) about 5 minutes or until hot. Stir in sugar, salt, eggs and vanilla. Beat briefly. Pour through sieve into 4 individual serving dishes and sprinkle with nutmeg. Stand in baking dish with hot water 1cm deep. Microwave on Medium (50% power) about 8-15 minutes or until centres are just set. (Cooking time varies.)

Moulded Caramel Custard

For 2 servings:
Caramel layer:
2 Tbsp sugar
2 tsp water

Custard:
¾ cup milk
1 Tbsp sugar
1 large egg
¼ tsp vanilla

Put 1 Tbsp of sugar and 1 tsp of water in two heat-resistant glass custard cups. Microwave on High (100% power) for 2-3 minutes, until light brown. (As soon as you smell caramel, stop cooking it!) Tilt custard cups to line with caramel. In a litre-sized measuring jug heat milk and sugar until very hot but not boiling (1-1½ minutes). Add egg and vanilla and beat until thoroughly mixed. Pour through a sieve into custard cups. Microwave on Defrost (30% power) for 4 minutes, or until custards have barely set. Reposition them once or twice, so they cook evenly. Refrigerate for 1 hour or longer. Unmould.

Note: At lower power levels waterbath is not necessary.

Cheesecake

For 8-10 servings:
Crust:
50g butter
1 cup biscuit crumbs
2 Tbsp sugar

In a medium-sized bowl microwave the butter on High (100% power) for 1½ minutes or until melted. Mix in biscuit crumbs and sugar. Line a 23cm pie dish with cling wrap. Press the mixture firmly into the lined dish and microwave on High for 1½ minutes. Set aside.

Filling:
2 cartons (250g each) cream cheese
¾ cup sugar
¼ tsp salt
2 Tbsp flour
¼ cup milk
½ tsp vanilla
finely grated rind of one lemon
2 Tbsp lemon juice
4 eggs

Soften uncovered cartons of cream cheese in the microwave on High (100% power) for 1 minute. Turn into a large mixing bowl or food processor. Mix briefly with sugar, salt, flour and milk. Add vanilla, lemon rind, juice and eggs. Microwave filling in a bowl for 4-10 minutes, or until mixture is evenly hot (but not set) stirring every minute after 3 minutes. Pour over crust and microwave on Medium (50% power) for 12-15 minutes or until set in the centre. Cool and refrigerate 2-3 hours. Before serving, spread with jam or fruit glaze.

Passionfruit Glaze

2-4 passionfruit
wine, orange juice or water
¼ cup sugar
2-3 tsp cornflour or custard powder

Scoop pulp from passionfruit into a half cup measure. Make up to ½ cup with wine, juice or water. Tip most of this liquid into a medium-sized bowl with the sugar, but reserve 2 Tbsp. Stir well, then microwave on High (100% power) 1½-2 minutes, until syrup boils. Add thickening to the remaining liquid, stirring to a smooth paste. Stir this into hot syrup. Heat again until transparent right through, about 1 minute, stirring twice. Pour glaze over cheesecake. A smaller amount of thickening produces a thinner glaze that dribbles deliciously down the sides of cut wedges.

Apple Layer Cake

For 6 servings:
Pastry:
¼ cup sugar
2 tsp cinnamon
3 cups flour
200g cold butter
1 egg
¼ cup cream
½ tsp microwave browning

Combine sugar and cinnamon. Put aside half of this mixture for topping. In a food processor, combine remaining sugar mixture and flour. Cut in the butter until it resembles coarse crumbs. Combine egg, cream and browning and add to the flour mixture. Blend until mixture holds together. Chill for 20 minutes. Divide into four parts. On floured baking paper roll out four 23cm circles. Cut out and remove a 6cm circle from the centre. Sprinkle each ring with 1 tsp of the sugar and cinnamon mixture. Place each ring of mixture on its paper on the turntable and microwave on High (100% power) for 2½-3 minutes or until lightly browned. Watch carefully to prevent burning.

Filling:
6 large apples, peeled and sliced
¾ cup sugar
¼ cup flour
1 tsp cinnamon

Mix ingredients in a large covered dish. Microwave on high (100% power) for 10-12 minutes or until tender and thickened.

To serve:
Layer pastry rings and warm apple mixture on serving plate, starting and finishing with pastry. Cut carefully. Top each serving with whipped cream.

Variation: Cook pastry in small squares. Layer three or four squares with apple for one serving.

Bread Pudding

Rich and sinfully delicious!

For 4 servings:
25g butter
75g very dry bread (2 bread rolls)
3/4 cup milk
1/4 cup cream or extra milk
1/2 cup sugar
1 egg
1 egg white
1 tsp vanilla
1/4 cup sultanas or currants
1/4 cup walnuts or almonds
1/4 tsp cinnamon
1/4 tsp mixed spice
1/4 tsp grated nutmeg

In a large bowl melt the butter on High (100% power) for 1-2 minutes. Add bread, broken into small pieces. Stir in milk (and cream if used), sugar, egg, egg white and vanilla. Press mixture to soften bread, then beat with fork to combine. Add the fruit, nuts and spices. The mixture should be firm enough to keep a rounded shape in 4 individual dishes. Microwave the dishes uncovered at Medium (50% power) for 8-10 minutes or until firm. Serve with rum or whisky sauce.

Sauce:
50g butter
3/4 cup icing sugar
1 egg yolk
2-3 Tbsp rum or whisky

In a medium-sized bowl melt the butter on High (100% power) for 1 minute. Beat in the icing sugar and egg yolk. Microwave for 30 seconds or until the liquid bubbles around the edges. Cool, then stir in whisky or rum.

Upside-Down Cake

Upside-down cakes cook best in lined ring-pans with straight sides.

For 6 servings:
Topping:
2 Tbsp butter
2-3 Tbsp golden syrup
6-8 pineapple rings
6-8 cherries

Line a 23cm round pan with a cut-open oven bag so topping will not stick to the pan. Place a glass in the centre. Melt butter in the pan on High (100% power) for about 30 seconds, then dribble the golden syrup evenly over the butter. Arrange the pineapple in a circle. Halve the cherries and place in and around pineapple rings.

Cake:
50g butter
1/2 cup brown sugar
1 tsp vanilla
1/2 tsp cinnamon
1 egg
1 1/4 cups flour
2 tsp baking powder
pineapple juice or milk

In a mixing bowl, melt the butter. Add the brown sugar, vanilla, cinnamon and egg and beat until light. Sift the flour and baking powder into the mixture with nearly half a cup of juice from the pineapple. Add extra juice and/or milk to make a soft drop batter. Do not overmix. Spoon batter over pineapple rings. Cover pan lightly with cling wrap. Stand pan on an inverted dinner plate. Microwave for about 6 minutes, until batter has set, or for more even cooking, microwave on Medium (50% power) for about 12 minutes. Leave for 5 minutes, remove the glass and invert onto serving plate.

Fruit Crumble

Microwaved fruit crumble does not turn golden brown, but it is so quick and easy.

For 4-6 servings:
4 cups sliced raw fruit

Or:
3 cups drained stewed fruit
1/2 cup rolled oats
1/2 cup white or brown sugar
1/4 cup wholemeal or plain flour
1 tsp mixed spice
50g cold butter
ground cloves

Put the prepared raw or cooked fruit in a microwave-proof 23cm pie plate or another shallow dish. Combine the remaining ingredients except the ground cloves. Cut in butter until crumbly. Sprinkle topping evenly over fruit, then sprinkle with the cloves. Microwave on High (100% power) for 8-12 minutes (or until fruit is tender). Leave 15-20 minutes and serve warm.

Steamed Carrot Pudding

A dark, well-flavoured pudding.

For 6 servings:
100g butter
2 cups finely grated carrots
1 egg
1 cup brown sugar
1 cup flour
3/4 tsp baking soda
1 tsp cinnamon
1 tsp mixed spice
1/2 cup sultanas

Melt butter in a mixing bowl on High (100% power) for about 1 1/2 minutes. Stir in carrots, egg and sugar. Sift in dry ingredients and add sultanas. Stir until mixed. The thickness of the mixture depends on the carrots. If very thin, stir in 1/4 cup flour. The final mixture should be thinner than a butter cake mixture. Pour into a small ring mould. Cover with a lid or plastic cling wrap. Microwave for about 7 minutes or until firm in centre. Leave to stand for 2 minutes then unmould.

"Encore" Steamed Pudding

The colour, texture and flavour of the pudding will vary, depending on the cake being "recycled".

2 cups (200g) crumbled, stale cake
½ cup flour
½ tsp baking soda
¼ cup white or brown sugar
50g cold butter
¼-½ cup sultanas or currants
¾-1 cup milk, juice, etc.

In a food processor or mixing bowl, crumble the cake finely. Add flour, soda and sugar. Mix thoroughly. Cut or rub in butter. Add dried fruit, if desired. Stir in enough liquid to make a batter wet enough to pour into a lightly sprayed or buttered small ring mould. Cover with cling wrap. Place the mould on an inverted dinner plate and microwave on High (100% power) for 5 minutes, or until firm. Leave to stand for 2-3 minutes, then unmould.

Golden Queen Pudding

For **4-6 servings**:
2 Tbsp butter
1 Tbsp custard powder
2 Tbsp peach syrup
¼ cup golden syrup
2-3 cooked peach halves
¼ cup walnut halves or pieces
2 cups Alison Holst's Baking Mix
2 Tbsp custard powder
1 cup milk

In a small microwave ring pan melt the butter, then add the first measure of custard powder, peach syrup and golden syrup. Microwave on High (100% power) for 1½ minutes, then place the peach halves (halved again), rounded side down, in the sauce. Sprinkle the walnuts between the peaches. With a fork, toss the baking mix

and custard powder together in a mixing bowl, then stir in the milk to form a drop-scone dough. Drop in spoonfuls, on top of the peaches and sauce.
Microwave, uncovered, on High (100% power) for 4-6 minutes, until firm close to the inner ring. Leave 2 minutes before turning out.
Note: For more even cooking, cover and microwave on Medium (50% power) for about 10 minutes, if preferred.

Marshmallow Pavlova

This doesn't have a crisp crust, but it has a lovely marshmallow texture.

4 egg whites
¼ tsp salt
1 cup castor sugar
1 tsp wine vinegar
1 tsp vanilla

In electric mixer, beat whites with salt until soft peaks form. Add sugar gradually, over 2-3 minutes, then vinegar and vanilla.
Pile meringue onto a flat plate. Stand this on an inverted plate. Microwave on High (100% power) for 3 minutes. Leave to stand in oven to cool or transfer to conventional oven and brown top under the grill. Leave to cool in the oven with the door ajar. When cold, decorate as desired.
Note: (a) Pavlova may split while baking. Splits close on standing. (b) Some syrup will leak from pavlova on standing.
Variation: Slide pavlova on top of a cooked pie.

Tamarillo Apple Pie

Cook this pie in four easy stages. The topping and filling are made before the pastry, then the assembled pie is cooked briefly.

For **6-8 servings**:
Topping:
50g cold butter
½ cup rolled oats
¼ cup flour
¼ cup sugar

In a medium-sized bowl or food processor, cut butter finely through other ingredients. Spread on a 23cm pie plate. Microwave on High (100% power) for 3 minutes. Transfer to paper.

Filling:
4 cups sliced apple
1 cup chopped peeled tamarillo
¾ cup sugar
¼ cup flour
½ tsp cinnamon

Mix ingredients in a large microwave dish. Cover and cook for 7-8 minutes or until tender and thick, stirring several times.

Crust:
60g cold butter
1 cup flour
about ¼ cup milk
4-6 drops gravy browning

Cut butter into flour in bowl or food processor. Mix milk and gravy browning or microwave browner until milk is light brown. Add to flour, a few drops at a time to make a stiff dough. Roll out thinly. Ease into pie dish. Fold back edge and decorate. Prick base all over. Microwave for 4-6 minutes, until middle looks dry. (Sides will subside a little.)
To combine: Pour filling into cooked crust and sprinkle cooked topping over pie. Cook 2 minutes or until edges start bubbling. Cool and serve with whipped cream.
Apple Pie
Proceed as above, without the tamarillo.

Baking

Baking

In less than the time it takes to heat a conventional oven, you can make and cook a microwaved cake, and have it eaten by several teenagers! You are unlikely to win prizes at shows with these cakes, but you can do a lot of family baking, especially things which can be eaten within twenty-four hours. Once you are an experienced microwave-cake baker you can produce some very good results. You may also produce some disappointing results, especially when you first start baking in your microwave.

Choosing the right mixture
For best colour through the cake, choose recipes which have some natural colour — brown sugar, spices, cocoa, citrus fruit juice, dried fruit, golden syrup and treacle.
To hide an unbrowned surface, add a cooked-on topping, icing or other decoration.
If you want a cake which will stay fresh and soft for several days, choose a recipe which includes grated fruit, vegetables or soaked grains. The brown bread, carrot and apple cakes here are especially good for this.
Cakes with a fairly high proportion of butter or oil usually microwave well.

Choose the best container
Cakes usually cook most evenly in ring containers with rounded corners at the bottom, and fairly straight sides.
For some mixtures you need a square shape. A 20cm square pyrex pan can produce good results if you mask its corners with foil and/or cover the surface during cooking. Loaf pans work well, too, if you mask their ends, and/or cover them. The mixture in the centre (especially bottom centre) cooks slowly. The outer edges of very large cakes cook slowly, too. Consider dividing a large mixture between two smaller containers. Total cooking time may well be the same.

Use the right techniques
Covered cakes rise higher, and cook more evenly. Use a lid, a sheet of greaseproof paper, a folded paper towel or vented plastic film, and see which works best for you.

Try the same mixture cooked in
(a) a covered ring pan
(b) a covered 20cm square pan
(c) A covered loaf pan
All are good, and produce different shapes and depths of mixture.
If you don't cover cakes tightly you will need to mask corners of square pans with foil, to stop them over-cooking.
You will often find baking cooks most evenly if it is raised from the bottom of the oven. Leave an inverted dinner plate or a microwave roasting pan in the oven when you bake.
In older ovens without turntables you may need to turn the baking pan at intervals, for most even cooking.

Do not undercook or overcook
To prevent uneven cooking cover the pan, lift container off bottom of oven, and lower the power level, increasing the cooking time to compensate.
At half the suggested power level a mixture takes about twice as long to cook, but cooks more evenly. Remember that cakes etc. keep cooking during the standing time after cooking. Allow for this. Overcooked cakes dry out on standing. Undercooked cakes have wet patches.
The surface of uncovered cake may appear damp and sticky even after the rest of the cake is cooked. Lift this off by pressing a paper towel on it.
When a cake is cooked it springs back and starts to shrink from the sides. A skewer comes out clean. The surface is not usually brown or crusty.

Preparing pans.
Techniques vary with individual pans and recipes. Always leave in pan during standing time. Some pans may need no preparation at all. Use oven bags, plastic film, greaseproof paper to line pans which stick. Use non-stick spray sparingly, or butter surface lightly. Never butter and flour pans. Experiment with buttering pan lightly then coating thinly with fine golden brown crumbs. Non-stick teflon liners are particularly useful for lining ring pans.

Brown Bread

This makes a well flavoured, heavy textured, unkneaded brown loaf which will remain moist for several days.

½ cup kibbled wheat
1 cup cold water
2 Tbsp treacle
1 tsp dried yeast granules
1 tsp sugar
½ cup warm water
½ cup rolled oats
1½ cups wholemeal flour
¾ cup flour
1½ tsp salt
1 Tbsp oil
½ cup milk
toasted sesame seeds (optional)

Measure the kibbled wheat into a fairly large plastic mixing bowl. Add the water and bring to the boil, about 4 minutes on High (100% power). Leave to stand 1 minute, then drain off the liquid, leaving the wheat in the bowl. Add the treacle. In a small container mix the yeast, sugar and lukewarm water. Leave to stand in a warm place until the surface bubbles. Without mixing, add the rolled oats, flours, salt, oil and milk into the kibbled wheat.
Tip in the bubbly yeast mixture and beat well to mix everything thoroughly. Heat in the microwave oven on Defrost (30% power) for 1 minute. Stir and feel temperature of dough. If quite cool, heat again until dough has warmed to body temperature. DO NOT OVERHEAT. Spoon dough into a loaf tin with its bottom and long sides lined with a strip of cling wrap. Moisten top and sprinkle with toasted sesame seeds or kibbled wheat. Cover surface lightly. Leave to rise in a warm steamy place or stand in the microwave oven. Microwave on Defrost (30% power) for 1 minute every 10 minutes. When risen to double its bulk after about an hour, stand loaf tin on an inverted dinner plate. Cook, uncovered, on Medium (50% power) for 16 minutes or until firm in the middle and cooked on the bottom. Remove from pan, turning in extra kibbled wheat and sesame seeds if desired.

Microwaved Scones

Scone mixtures rise well and cook very quickly, but are not brown and crusty. They are best made with colourful toppings, or as pinwheels, with spicy fillings. You can colour the surface using microwave browning spray, if you like, but I prefer additions like those used in the following recipe.

Cinnamon Scone Ring

Both the topping and filling used here provide the colour and texture lacking in plain microwaved scone dough. First mix topping.

Topping:
1 Tbsp butter
2 Tbsp golden syrup
2 Tbsp chopped walnuts

In a small ring pan melt butter, 30-40 seconds on High (100% power). Tilt pan to coat bottom evenly. Drizzle golden syrup over bottom and sides. Add chopped walnuts. Next mix scone dough.

Scone Dough:
2 cups Alison Holst's Baking Mix about ¾ cup milk

Add enough milk to baking mix to make a soft dough. Knead lightly 5-6 times, then roll out to form a rectangle 30cm x 20cm.

Filling:
2 Tbsp butter, melted
2 Tbsp chopped walnuts
1 tsp cinnamon
2 Tbsp brown sugar

Brush dough evenly with melted butter. Combine walnuts, cinnamon and brown sugar and sprinkle evenly over the dough. Roll up, starting with a long side. Cut roll into 8 slices. Arrange, cut side down, on the prepared topping in the pan. Cover pan with cling wrap. Cook for 6-7 minutes, or until dough nearest the ring insert feels firm. Leave to stand in pan for 2 minutes, then turn out on plate and serve immediately, buttered or plain.
Note: Replace baking mix and milk with your own scone mixture made with 2 cups flour, if preferred.

Microwaved Muffins

Many muffin recipes microwave well. Choose recipes with some ingredients which colour the batter. Take care not to overfill the muffin pans, since muffins rise well, but spread if they go over the top. Eat while warm, halved, with colourful spreads, if colour is pale.

Raisin Muffins

If you make a muffin mixture a little firmer than usual, it won't flatten when microwaved. These are best eaten within an hour of cooking — not usually a problem!

For 8-12 muffins:
1 cup wholemeal flour
2 Tbsp brown sugar
1½ tsp baking powder
½ tsp salt
½ cup raisins or sultanas
50g butter, melted
¼ cup golden syrup
1 egg

Mix the flour, sugar, baking powder and salt in a medium sized bowl. Stir thoroughly with a fork to blend. Add raisins. Melt the butter on High (100% power) for about 50 seconds until liquid but not hot. Add golden syrup. Microwave again until warm enough to mix easily, then add egg. Mix with a fork to combine. Stir liquid into dry ingredients. Stir only enough to moisten everything. Spoon into microwave cupcake pans (no lining or greasing should be necessary), filling each cup no

more than half full. Microwave for 2-3 minutes, or until centres are just dry. Leave 2 minutes, then carefully loosen and remove.

Variations:
(a) Replace syrup with treacle for darker colour. Add spices to suit.
(b) Replace raisins with chopped, drained cooked fruit or ripe bananas.
(c) Add 2 Tbsp milk for moister, flat-topped muffins.

Gingerbread

This light-coloured gingerbread is best buttered and served within half an hour of baking. Serve leftovers warmed for dessert with Lemon Sauce (see page 104).

75g butter, melted
½ cup golden syrup
¼ cup brown sugar
2 Tbsp boiling water
2 eggs
1¼ cups flour
½ tsp baking soda
1 tsp ground ginger
½ tsp cinnamon
¼ tsp ground cloves

In a fairly large bowl melt butter on High (100% power) for 45 seconds. Add golden syrup, heat for 30

seconds longer. Measure sugar, water and egg on top of this, and stir with a fork or rotary beater until thoroughly blended. Measure dry ingredients into a sieve standing over the bowl. Shake in, stir with a rubber scraper until combined. Very lightly butter microwave ring pan, or line with non-stick teflon liner, or snipped greaseproof paper ring. Pour in mixture and cover with plastic film or paper towel. Cook on medium-high (70% power) for 6-10 minutes, or until centre springs back. (Gingerbread in paper-lined loaf pan cooks in 8-10 minutes, but is harder to cook evenly).
Serve warm.
Note: This gingerbread dries out several hours after cooking.

Crunchy Apple Cake

This is an excellent microwave cake. It has an interesting crunchy topping, a good colour and a moist texture. It keeps well, too.
Topping:
25g butter, melted
½ cup rolled oats
¼ cup brown sugar
1 tsp cinnamon
1 tsp allspice

Melt the butter on High (100% power) for about 30 seconds. Add remaining topping ingredients, stir to blend, then put aside on a paper towel or in another container.

Cake:
125g butter, melted
2 tsp cinnamon
1 tsp allspice
¼ tsp ground cloves
1 tsp salt
1 cup brown sugar
1 egg
2 apples, grated
1½ cups flour
1 tsp baking soda

Mix the cake in the same bowl. Melt the butter for about 1 minute. Stir in the spices, salt, sugar and egg. Add the grated apple, stir again, then add the sifted flour and baking soda, stirring just enough to blend everything. Spread mixture into a 23cm square or round pan. Sprinkle topping evenly over the surface. Microwave, uncovered, on Medium (50% power) for 20-30 minutes or until the centre is firm. Shield corners during first 10 minutes, if desired.
Note: Cook in a round pan with glass in the middle at a high power level for a shorter cooking time, if desired.

Oaty Squares

Popular with all age groups!

100g butter
¼ cup (packed) brown sugar
¼ cup sugar
2 cups rolled oats
½ cup coconut or finely chopped
    nuts
1 tsp vanilla
¼ cup peanut butter
½ cup chocolate chips

In mixing bowl or microwave casserole dish, melt butter on High (100% power) for 45 seconds. Stir in sugars, rolled oats, coconut or nuts, and vanilla. Press into a 20cm pan lined with baking paper. Cook 3 minutes or until bubbling all over. Watch that mixture does not start to burn in the middle. In same mixing bowl heat the peanut butter and chocolate chips for 1½ minutes until they will mix together smoothly. Stir together and spread over oaty mixture. Cool.

Chewy Fudge Squares

For this recipe use half the Pastry recipe on page 109.

cooked crust
1 can (400g) condensed milk
1 cup chocolate morsels
few drops rum essence or
    ½ tsp vanilla essence
¼ cup almonds, slivered

Roll out the pastry so that it is bigger than the baking dish (about 17cm square or 15 x 20cm.) Place flat, on baking paper and prick well. Bake on High (100% power) for 3-4 minutes or until just firm. Cut to fit baking pan, leaving paper intact on 2 sides so it can be lifted easily into baking dish. Heat condensed milk in mixing bowl or casserole dish for 1½ minutes. Stir in chocolate morsels until they melt, then add essence. Pour onto baked crust. Cook for 2 minutes. Sprinkle with almonds and bake 1 minute longer or until barely firm in centre. Cool, and lift out square, still on its paper before cutting into squares. Squares harden on cooling.

Brownies

Brownies are an American favourite — not biscuits, but a chocolate slice popular with young and old. Their colour is rich and brown.

100g butter
2 eggs
1 cup sugar
1 tsp vanilla
¾ cup flour
¼ cup cocoa
1 tsp baking powder
¼-½ cup nuts (optional)

In a medium-sized bowl melt the butter on High (100% power) for 1½ minutes. Stir in the eggs, sugar, and vanilla. Beat well with a fork or rubber scraper. Stir in the sifted dry ingredients and nuts, if desired. Do not overmix. Spread mixture in a 20cm square or round pan lined with cling wrap or with the bottom lined with greaseproof paper. Cover or shield corners. Microwave 5-7 minutes. Take brownies from oven as soon as the centre is dry. Look at mixture every half minute after 4 minutes, to make sure it does not overcook. Cool in pan. Dredge with icing sugar and cut into wedges when cold.
Note: (a) This makes slightly chewy brownies. Add ¼ cup extra flour for firmer, drier brownies.
(b) Overcooked brownies are hard and dry. Use them for crumbs, for making truffles, etc.
Variation: Sprinkle ½ cup chocolate morsels over surface before baking.

Date Bars

Filling:
2 cups dates, chopped
½ cup water
¼ cup sugar
¼ cup lemon juice

Base:
100g butter
½ cup brown sugar
1 cup rolled oats
1 cup flour

Place all the filling ingredients in a medium-sized bowl. Microwave on High (100% power) for 4-5 minutes, until fairly thick when stirred. Combine base ingredients with a food processor or pastry blender to make a crumbly mixture. Keep one cupful aside and press rest into a lightly buttered 20cm

square baking dish. Microwave on Medium (50% power) for 5 minutes. Spread date filling on base. Sprinkle with reserved mixture. Microwave uncovered on High (100% power) for 5 minutes. Cool and cut in small squares or rectangles.

Peanut Butter Squares

100g butter
½ cup peanut butter
1 cup biscuit crumbs
1 cup icing sugar
about 6 drops almond essence
¼ tsp vanilla
½ cup chcoolate morsels
2 tsp butter

In a large bowl microwave on High (100% power) the butter (cut into cubes), and the peanut butter (in 4-5 blobs) for 2 minutes. Mix and blend thoroughly. Stir in crumbs, icing sugar and essences. Mix well. Press into loaf pan lined with baking paper. In another dish, melt chocolate and second measure of butter in the microwave for 1-2 minutes, or until the two can be mixed together smoothly. Add vanilla and spread on top of peanut butter mixture. Cool before cutting into small squares.

Orange Snacking Cake

Although this may be cooked in a loaf tin, I like it best as a flatter, thin cake, cut in pieces and served straight from its baking pan.

1 orange, grated rind and juice
water
1 egg
¼ cup sour cream
50g very soft butter
½ cup brown sugar
1 cup plus 2 Tbsp cake or plain
  flour
½ tsp baking soda

Grate rind from orange. Reserve ½ tsp for the icing and put the rest in a bowl. Squeeze juice. Reserve 1 Tbsp for the icing. Make the rest of the juice up to ½ cup with water. Combine with the rind and the remaining ingredients. Mix only until blended (about 10 seconds in a food processor). Turn into a 20cm square pan. Cover with a lid, greaseproof paper or cling wrap. Elevate on an inverted plate. Cook on Medium-High (70% power) for 7 minutes or until just firm in centre. Uncover. Leave to stand about 5 minutes, then ice.

Icing:
reserved rind and juice
2 tsp butter
1 cup icing sugar

Heat butter, reserved rind and juice for 10 seconds in the microwave. Add icing sugar. Beat until smooth. Spread over the warm or cooled cake.

Chocolate Cake

50g butter, melted
2 eggs
1 cup brown sugar
½ cup milk

1 cup flour
3 Tbsp cocoa
½ tsp baking soda
½ tsp cream of tartar

Melt butter in a medium-sized bowl on High (100% power) for about 1 minute. Add eggs and sugar and beat with a rotary beater until thick and creamy. Add milk and sifted dry ingredients. Beat again briefly, stopping as soon as ingredients are combined. Pour into a small ring pan which has been lightly sprayed or buttered. Cover pan with vented cling wrap. Microwave on Medium-High (70% power) for about 6-10 minutes or until firm near ring. Leave to stand for 3-4 minutes, then unmould onto flat plate. Ice when cold.
Variations: Make cake in a loaf pan or in a 20cm square pan. Cover during cooking, or shield corners.

Chocolate Icing

1 Tbsp cocoa
2 Tbsp water
2 tsp butter
1½ cups sifted icing sugar

Mix cocoa and water to a smooth paste. Heat cocoa on High (100% power) for 1-1½ minutes, until dark brown and thick. Add the butter, then stir in the sifted icing sugar. Add extra liquid only after the icing sugar is mixed, if necessary.

Banana Cake

125g butter, melted
1 cup brown sugar
1 Tbsp wine vinegar
2 eggs
2-3 very ripe bananas, mashed
1 cup wholemeal flour
¾ cup flour
1 tsp baking soda
¼ cup milk

In a fairly large mixing bowl melt the butter on High (100% power) for 1½ minutes. Add the sugar, vinegar and eggs, then beat with a fork or rotary beater until well mixed. Stir in the mashed bananas. Sprinkle the wholemeal flour over the surface. Add the flour and baking soda, sifted together, and the milk. Fold everything together, using a rubber scraper. Turn into a paper-lined or lightly buttered ring pan. Microwave on Medium-High (70% power) for 10-12 minutes, or until centre is firm. Ice with Lemon Butter Icing or with Cream Cheese Icing, and sprinkle with walnuts if desired.

Cream Cheese Icing

2 Tbsp cream cheese
1 Tbsp butter
½ tsp vanilla
1½ cups sifted icing sugar

Put cream cheese, butter and vanilla in a medium-sized bowl. Microwave on High (100% power) 20-30 seconds until cream cheese and butter are very soft. Add icing sugar and mix with a knife until smooth and creamy. Add a little milk or icing sugar if mixture is too thick or thin. Spread on slightly warm cake.

Carrot Cake

This is one of my favourite microwave cakes. When it is cooked in a good quality, smooth pan with a lid, no lining is necessary.

2 cups finely grated carrot
2 eggs
1 cup sugar
¾ cup oil
1 tsp vanilla
1¼ cups flour
2-3 tsp cinnamon
2-3 tsp mixed spice
1 tsp baking soda
½ tsp salt

Grate carrots finely and put aside. Mix eggs, sugar, oil, and vanilla in a food processor until smooth. Add carrot and remaining ingredients. (Add larger amounts of spices for a darker, spicier cake.) Process enough to combine everything thoroughly, but do not overmix. Turn mixture into a 10 cup capacity ring pan. If pan has a tendency to stick, line it first with strips of plastic cling film. Cover pan with a lid or plate. Microwave on High (100% power) for about 8 minutes or until top and bottom look just dry and centre springs back. Turn out and cool. Ice with a lemon butter icing and garnish with chopped walnuts.

Lemon Butter Icing

1 Tbsp butter
1½ Tbsp lemon juice
1½ cups sifted icing sugar
½ tsp finely grated lemon rind
   (optional)

Put butter, lemon rind and juice in a medium-sized bowl. Microwave on high (100% power) for 20 seconds, or until butter is soft. Add icing sugar and mix with a knife until smooth and creamy. Spread on slightly warm cake.

Cheesecake Tarts

1 Tbsp butter
½ cup malt biscuit crumbs
1 can (400g) sweetened
   condensed milk
2 eggs, lightly beaten
6 Tbsp lemon juice
grated rind of 1 lemon
about 20 paper cupcake liners

In a small bowl melt butter on High (100% power) for 30 seconds. Stir in crumbs. (Mixture will be fairly dry.) In another, bigger bowl, mix together the condensed milk, eggs, lemon juice and finely grated lemon rind.
Place 1 rounded household teaspoon of crumbs in each of 15 cupcake liners. Put 5 or 6 of these into microwave cupcake pans. Press crumbs evenly, then top with 2-3 tablespoons of the filling.
Microwave on Medium (50% power) until filling is firm in centre,

about 2-3 minutes. Lift from pan and cool. Cook other tarts as above. Refrigerate or keep in cool place up to 48 hours. Serve topped with whipped cream and a cherry, strawberry, sliced kiwifruit or other fresh berries.
Note: 6 Tbsp equals ⅜ cup.

Cathedral Window Cake

This cake is mainly nuts and glacé fruit, held together by a small amount of cake batter. When sliced thinly and held up to the light, it resembles a stained glass window.

1½ cups Brazil nuts
½ cup almonds
½ cup cashew nuts
½ cup red cherries
½ cup mixed cherries
1½ cups glacé fruit, e.g.
   pineapple, mangoes
½ cup sultanas
½ cup sticky raisins
¾ cup flour
½ cup brown sugar
½ tsp baking powder
¼ tsp salt
2 eggs
½ tsp vanilla

Measure the nuts, fruit and dry ingredients into a large bowl, reserving some for decoration. Cut up large pieces of fruit. Mix eggs and vanilla until thoroughly combined and add to other ingredients. Add a little gravy

browning to darken mixture if desired. Mix thoroughly by hand. Line a flat-bottomed ring pan with baking paper or with a non-stick teflon liner. Press mixture firmly into pan. Decorate top with reserved cherries etc. Cover cake with vented plastic film.
Stand ring pan on an inverted plate. Microwave on Defrost (30% power) for 45-75 minutes or until centre feels firm, and cake dough seems cooked.
Store, loosely wrapped in greaseproof paper not in an airtight container, up to 3 months.
Note: If cake overcooks, store it in a plastic bag with spirits or sherry sprinkled liberally over it, in refrigerator until it softens.

Drinks, etc.

Drinks, etc

Your microwave is very useful for making and heating drinks. You save time and effort and eliminate washing up because the liquid is heated in the glass, cup, mug or paper cup that you will drink from. The handle will stay cool enough to hold, while the liquid heats to the temperature you want.
You heat only as much water as you need, instead of heating more to cover the jug element as well. You save the most time and electricity when you heat water for 1 or 2 drinks.

Chart for Boiling Cold Tap Water
1 cup — 2½-3 minutes
2 cups — 5-6 minutes
3 cups — 7-8½ minutes
4 cups — 9-11 minutes

For heating more than 2 cups of liquid, you may find conventional methods faster.
The times quoted in the following recipes are for room temperature liquids. The times will vary slightly with the size of the cup, mug or glass you use. If you take liquid from the refrigerator, it will take a little longer to heat. If you use warm or hot tap water, the time will be shorter.

Tips about different liquids
Liquids with a high fat or sugar content heat faster. A cup of creamy milk will heat faster than a cup of low fat milk, which will heat faster than water. Half a cup of liquid will heat faster than a full cup.
With practice you will be able to judge the times precisely. You may also like to work out heating positions in your oven, putting longer heating drinks nearer the outside of the turntable and faster heating drinks nearer the centre. Most people find that they never heat milk in a saucepan after they have a microwave oven!

Which Cups, Mugs, Jugs?
Once you have your microwave, put aside any mugs or cups which you cannot use in it.
Cups with gold or silver trims are not suitable. Pottery with a high metal content may not microwave well. (Refer to the test on page 7). As well as individual mugs, you will find glass measuring cups and jugs, and plastic, heat resistant glass and china jugs useful for making and heating drinks.
An unbreakable 1 litre hard, clear plastic jug is useful for hot or cold drinks, and for both heating and serving.
You may find a small metal whisk useful if you want to make one-cup quantities of cocoa, etc.
Don't use tea or coffee makers with metal bands, screws or bolts.

Warming up drinks
To warm up cups of tea or coffee that have become cold, just put the cup into the microwave on High (100% power) for about 1-1½ minutes. Be careful not to let your drink boil or you will alter its flavour, especially if you have added milk to it.

Microwaving cold drinks
You may not immediately think of using your microwave oven for making cold drinks! The microwave is especially useful when you want to make a small quantity of sugar syrup, concentrated tea, coffee, etc. in order to dilute and cool it fast, so that it can be drunk immediately. You can often make the syrup in the jug, mug or glass in which you serve the drink.

Tea, Instant Coffee and Soup
Nearly fill your cup or mug with water. Heat on High (100% power) for 1-3 minutes. (Hot water will boil more quickly than cold water.) The size of the cup and the number you are heating at once will also make a difference to the time required. Two cups take a little less than twice the time of one, and three cups take nearly three times as long, etc.) As soon as the water boils, remove the cup and add a tea bag, a teaspoon of instant coffee, or the desired amount of soup mix.

Coffee from ground beans
Make up the quantity of coffee you drink daily, using your favourite method. Heat a cup of the coffee in the microwave on High (100% power) for about 1½ minutes whenever you want hot coffee. Two or three cup quantities can be heated in glass or china jugs as long as the container has no metal decoration or screws, etc., is not too tall and narrow or is not constricted at the top. (Do not let the coffee boil as the pressure of bubbling liquid can break tall, narrow necked containers.)

Heating Milk
Cold milk will take longer to heat than room temperature milk. Overheating the milk will cause it to boil onto the floor of the oven, so the first time you heat milk in your favourite mug, watch it carefully and record the time taken to reach drinking temperature. A 250mls cup of refrigerated milk microwaved on High (100% power) takes about 1¾ minutes to heat to drinking temperature.

Warming Baby's Bottle
Heat the bottle with or without the teat attached. Half a cup (125mls) of refrigerated milk microwaved on High (100% power) warms in about 25 seconds. Be sure to shake the bottle after heating and ALWAYS test the temperature of the milk on the inside of your wrist before giving it to a baby.

Heating Soup
Make soup according to your favourite recipe and store it in the refrigerator, taking out a cup at a time to heat in the microwave on High (100% power) until warm. For longer storage, freeze soup in microwave containers, defrost in the microwave, stirring several times as soup thaws. Then heat required amount.

Milky Coffee and Drinking Chocolate
Add the instant coffee or powdered chocolate before heating the milk. Hot milk may froth up if the powder is added to hot liquid.

Cocoa

For the best flavour, boil the cocoa, sugar and water before you add the milk.
For 1 serving:
1 tsp cocoa
2 tsp sugar
¼ cup water
¾ cup milk

In a mug stir the cocoa and sugar together carefully so the finished drink will have no lumps. Add the water and microwave on High (100% power) for 1 minute. Add the milk, stir well and microwave about 45 seconds, to desired hotness. For a treat, drop 1-2 marshmallows into the hot cocoa.

Hot Mocha

This is an interesting winter drink for children or adults. Alter the proportion of ingredients if you like.

For 1 large serving:
1½ Tbsp drinking chocolate
1-2 tsp instant coffee
1 cup milk
whipped cream
cinnamon or chocolate curls

Mix drinking chocolate, instant coffee, sugar and milk in a mug. Microwave on High (100% power) until steaming (1½ minutes). Top with lightly whipped cream and add a pinch of cinnamon or chocolate curls.

Irish Coffee

These days almost any whisky-coffee mixture is called Irish coffee, so please yourself when you make it, using strong, freshly made coffee or instant granules. Sweeten the coffee, the cream, or both.

For 1 serving:
½ cup freshly made strong coffee
or 2 tsp instant coffee dissolved in
½ cup hot water
1-2 tsp sugar
1-2 Tbsp whisky
lightly whipped cream

Mix all ingredients except cream in a microwave-proof mug or glass. Microwave on High (100% power) for 45 seconds to 1 minute, until very hot. Stir to mix sugar. Then carefully pour cream onto the surface. Drink without stirring.

Hot Egg Nog

For a pick-me-up or a meal in a glass, this is hard to beat.

For 1 large or 2 small servings:
1 egg, separated
1 cup milk
3-4 tsp brown or white sugar
few drops of vanilla
¼ tsp freshly grated nutmeg

Separate egg into two small bowls. To the yolk add milk, 1½ tsp sugar, vanilla, and most of the nutmeg. Mix with a rotary beater and microwave on High (100% power) for 2½-3 minutes, until bubbling around the edges. Beat the mixture again briefly, and then microwave for a few seconds until it bubbles again. In the meantime rinse beater and beat egg white until foamy. Add remaining sugar and beat until peaks turn over. Tip most of the egg white into the hot mixture and beat briefly. Pour mixture into one or two mugs or glasses, top with remaining egg white and sprinkle with nutmeg. Serve hot.

Variation: For adults, replace vanilla with 1 Tbsp rum, whisky or brandy if desired.

Hot Buttered Rum

This is a welcoming drink for a cold winter evening.

For 1 large serving:
1 cup apple juice
cinnamon stick (optional)
2-3 cloves (optional)
curl of lemon or orange rind (optional)
2-4 Tbsp rum
½-1 tsp butter

In microwave-proof mug combine juice, spices and rind (if used). Microwave on High (100% power) for 2 minutes or until hot but not boiling. Add rum and butter. Stir and serve with a cinnamon stick.

Blackcurrant Cup

Although blackcurrant and wine mixtures are often served cold, they are delicious when hot, too. Sweeten to taste.

For 2 servings:
1 cup white wine
1 Tbsp blackcurrant cordial (or cassis)
1 strip orange peel
sugar (optional)

Combine ingredients in one or two heat-proof mugs. Heat on High (100% power) for 2 minutes or until hot but not boiling. Taste, add a little sugar if desired, and serve with orange wedges.

Hot Toddy

This makes a wonderful nightcap and is widely acclaimed as a cold cure. Whatever its medicinal properties, it is sure to make you feel better!

For 1 serving:
1 Tbsp brown sugar
thinly peeled rind and juice from half a lemon
½ cup (125ml) water
1-2 slices root ginger (optional)
1-2 Tbsp whisky (optional)

Measure sugar, lemon rind, juice and water into a microwave-proof glass or mug. Add ginger if desired. Heat on High (100% power) for 45 seconds or until hot but not boiling. Stir and then add whisky to taste.

Fresh Lemonade

Quickly made, this drink is deliciously refreshing. Make it fizzy or not.

For 2 servings:
1 lemon, rind and juice
2 Tbsp sugar
½ cup water
ice
extra water or soda water

Peel lemon, removing only coloured rind. In a measuring cup microwave lemon rind, juice and sugar on High (100% power) for 2 minutes or until sugar dissolves when stirred. Stir in ½ cup cold water. Pour liquid over ice in two tall glasses. Top up with extra water or soda water. Stir, garnish and serve.

Raspberry Soda

This brightly coloured drink may be made using whatever berries are in season.

For 6-8 servings:
2 cups raspberries
¼ cup water
¼ cup sugar
½ tsp citric acid

Crush the berries with the water using a potato masher, fork or food processor. Microwave in a wide-bottom bowl on High (100% power) for 2 minutes. Add sugar and citric acid and microwave for 2 minutes longer or until hot enough to dissolve sugar. Stir once or twice. Strain to remove berries, shaking strainer. Pour ¼ cup syrup over ice in tall glasses. Fill glasses with ¾-1 cup soda water (or water). Refrigerate remaining syrup up to 2 weeks. (Note: Use frozen berries if desired.)

Tangelo Cooler

Tangelos give this drink a very definite colour and flavour, but you can use oranges instead, if you like.

For 4-6 servings:
2 tangelos, rind and juice
½ cup sugar
½ tsp citric acid
¼ cup water

Grate or peel the coloured skin from the tangelos. Put into a 1 litre jug with the sugar, citric acid and water. Microwave on High (100% power) about 2 minutes or until mixture boils. Stir until sugar dissolves. Add tangelo juice and fill to 1 litre level with cold water. Pour over ice cubes. (**Variation**: Measure equal portions of recipe and white wine.)

Kiwi Smoothie

For a really interesting, smooth and creamy drink, combine kiwifruit with coconut cream.

About 4 servings:
2 tsp grated fresh root ginger
¼ cup sugar
½ cup water
1 kiwifruit
½ cup coconut cream

Mix ginger, sugar and water. Microwave in a measuring cup on High (100% power) for 2-3 minutes or until boiling briskly. Remove skin and core from kiwifruit. Chop roughly in a food processor with hot ginger syrup and coconut cream until smooth. Shake through a sieve to remove seeds. Serve over ice with equal quantities of either apple juice or white wine. Garnish as desired.

Tomato Juice

For the best flavour, use ripe red tomatoes from your garden.

For 1 litre:
1kg quartered tomatoes
1 onion, chopped
2 tsp sugar
1 tsp salt
½ tsp celery salt
basil to taste
freshly ground pepper

Put all ingredients together into large covered dish and microwave on High (100% power) for 10 minutes. Purée in food processor and shake through strainer, discarding pulp. Cool, taste and adjust seasoning. Refrigerate in covered container up to 2-3 days.

Iced Lemon Tea

This refreshing hot weather drink can be made with a small amount of hot liquid.

For 2 servings:
1½ cups water
1 tea bag
3 slices of lemon
juice of remaining lemon
ice
mint sprigs

Heat ½ cup water in a measuring cup until it boils rapidly (about 2 minutes). Immediately drop in tea bag and one slice of lemon. Leave 2 minutes and then remove (and squeeze) tea bag. Add juice squeezed from lemon after removing 3 slices. Add sugar to taste (2-3 teaspoons). Add remaining water. Pour over ice cubes and mint sprigs in two glasses topping up with extra water if necessary. Garnish with remaining lemon slices.

123

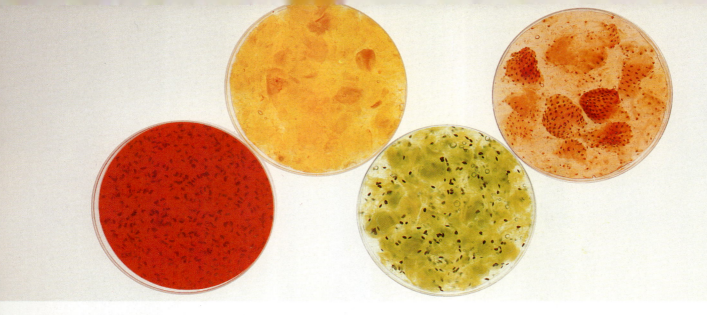

Jams and Pickles

Small amounts of jam cook well in microwave ovens. The jam never sticks or burns on the bottom and has a good fruit flavour and bright colour.

Because jams get very hot, it is important to use containers which will not soften or melt at high heat. Use larger bowls or casserole dishes, since small amounts of jam can bubble up surprisingly high. Bubbling stops as soon as oven door is opened and is more manageable if lower power levels are used. Lower the power level to 70% or 50% and increase times, if necessary.

Do not seal before end point is reached or jam may form mould on top during storage.

To test for setting, pour about 2 teaspoons of jam onto a cold, dry saucer. Stand in a cool place for 2-3 minutes. When the jam is ready, its surface should wrinkle when you draw your finger over it.

Modify your own jam recipes, using these as a guide.

If jam and pickles are to be eaten within a few weeks, do not seal the jars but keep them in the refrigerator. For longer storage or for gifts, seal the preserves in clean jars which have been heated thoroughly and have laquered metal screw-on lids.

Wash jars thoroughly, then:

(a) Heat in conventional oven at 140C for 15 minutes or
(b) Boil in a large bowl or saucepan in water to cover or
(c) Quarter fill jars with water and microwave until water boils for 1 minute.

To sterilise metal lids, drop them in a container of boiling water. Do not microwave.

Pour hot jams and pickles into hot jars to within 1 cm of top. Screw on hot lid immediately.

Raspberry Jam

For best flavour make small batches of this jam at regular intervals.

For 2 small jars:
500g raspberries, fresh or frozen
500g sugar

In a large, uncovered high heat-resistant bowl or casserole dish microwave the raspberries on High (100% power) until they boil vigorously, about 5 minutes. Add sugar and stir until most of it dissolves. Heat for 6-8 minutes, stirring every 2 minutes until a little jam sets on a cold saucer. Remove from oven. Beat with a rotary beater for about 1 minute. Pour into prepared jars and seal.

Apricot Jam

500g apricots
2 Tbsp lemon juice
sugar

Halve apricots, then cut each half into four quarters. Place in a large high temperature-resistant bowl or high-sided casserole. Add the lemon juice. Microwave on High (100% power) for 5-8 minutes, stirring when fruit bubbles around the edge of the dish, and heating again until whole surface boils vigorously. Measure the volume of fruit, and add three quarters of a cup of sugar to each cup of fruit. Stir thoroughly. Cook 5-10 minutes, until a little jam sets. (See test.) Pour into prepared jars and seal.

Kiwifruit Jam

Serve this for breakfast, instead of marmalade.

500g prepared kiwifruit
1/4 cup lemon juice
2 cups sugar

Remove skins of kiwifruit, either by peeling or by halving and scooping out centres. Cut lengthwise and remove central core and the area close to it containing most seeds. Weigh fruit after this preparation. Mash with a potato masher. Microwave fruit and lemon juice in a large, high heat-resistant bowl until mixture boils vigorously, about 6 minutes. Stir in sugar, dissolving it as much as possible. Cook about 8 minutes longer until a little jam sets. (See test.) Add enough green food colouring to produce a pleasing green colour. Pour into prepared jars and seal.

Strawberry Jam

Ever popular with adults and children alike.
500g strawberries
3 cups sugar
1 tsp tartaric acid

Halve or quarter large berries. In a large high heat-resistant microwave bowl or high-sided casserole dish heat on High (100% power) until berries bubble around edge of container. Add sugar and heat again for 6 minutes, stirring after 2 and 4 minutes. Add tartaric acid and heat again for 6-10 minutes or until a little jam sets. (See test.) Pour into prepared jars and seal.

Christmas Pickle

This pretty pickle is especially good with cold meat.
For 2 medium jars:
2 cups diced cucumber
1 Tbsp plain salt
1 onion, chopped
1 small red pepper, chopped
¾ cup sugar
¼ tsp celery seed
¼ tsp mustard seed
½ cup wine or cider vinegar
1 Tbsp cornflour

Halve cucumber lengthwise, scoop out and discard seeds, using a spoon. Cube unpeeled flesh, sprinkle with salt and leave for 30 minutes, stirring occasionally. Rinse and drain, discarding liquid. Combine cucumber with onion and red pepper in a large, flat-bottomed casserole or batter-bowl. Add flavourings and vinegar. Microwave on High (100% power) for 5-6 minutes, until mixture boils vigorously. Thicken with cornflour mixed to a paste with extra vinegar. Heat again until bubbling, 2-3 minutes. Pour into prepared jars and seal.

Tamarillo Chutney

Deep in colour with an interesting flavour, this is a good all-purpose chutney.

For 1 medium jar:
3 large or 4 small tamarillos
1 apple, chopped
1 onion, finely chopped
¾ cup brown sugar
¼ tsp mixed spice
¼ tsp salt
¼ cup vinegar

Cut stems from tamarillos and halve lengthwise. Place, cut surface down, on flat-bottomed high-sided casserole or high heat-resistant bowl.
Microwave on High (100% power) for 4 minutes or until skins may be lifted off fruit easily. Mash fruit with potato masher. Add finely chopped apple and onion, sugar, spice, salt and vinegar. Cover and cook for 10 minutes. Uncover and cook 6 minutes longer until fairly thick. Pour into prepared jars and seal.

Bread and Butter Pickles

A favourite in sandwiches, on crackers, with cheese and meat.

2 cups sliced cucumber
1 cup sliced onion
2 Tbsp plain salt
¾ cup white vinegar
¾ cup sugar
1 tsp mustard seed
1 tsp celery seed
¼ tsp turmeric

Slice hothouse cucumber(s) to fill a 2 cup measure. Slice onions thinly and measure. Combine vegetables, sprinkle with salt and leave 30 minutes. Drain and rinse well. In a large high heat-resistant bowl or casserole, combine white vinegar, sugar and flavourings. Microwave on High (100% power) for 2 minutes. Stir to dissolve sugar. Heat again until boiling rapidly. Add vegetables, stir well, heat until bubbling around the edge. Seal (see general method) or pour into large jar without sealing and refrigerate.

Parliament Pickle

A good all-purpose pickle, a cross between mustard pickle and tomato relish.

250g firm red tomatoes
1 medium cucumber (250g)
1 small onion
¾ cup finely sliced celery
1 Tbsp salt
¾ cup sugar
2 tsp dry mustard
2 tsp turmeric
2 Tbsp flour
½ cup white vinegar

Blanch tomatoes by pouring boiling water over them, leaving them to stand for 1 minute, draining them and covering with cold water. Halve, peel, discard seeds and cube flesh finely.
Peel cucumber only if skin is tough. Halve, scoop out, discard seeds, and cube, like tomatoes. Mix cucumber, onion and celery in a plastic or glass bowl and the tomatoes in another. Sprinkle both with the salt and leave to stand for an hour stirring occasionally. Mix sugar, mustard, turmeric and flour in a large microwave bowl. Add vinegar and stir until smooth. Microwave on High (100% power) for 3 minutes or until mixture thickens and boils. Drain and rinse both lots of vegetables. Add to thickened vinegar, heat again 3-4 minutes, or until boiling again. Pour into prepared jars and seal.

Fabulous Fudge

This is such delicious, soft, smooth fudge that you should experiment with the cooking time until you get it exactly right for your oven and dish. If you have to beat the fudge for too long, increase the cooking time by 30 seconds, next time.

100g butter
1 cup sugar
¼ cup golden syrup
1 can (400g) sweetened condensed milk
1 tsp vanilla

Mix all ingredients except vanilla in a 22cm flat-bottomed casserole or a batter bowl resistant to high heat. Microwave on High (100% power) for 7-9 minutes, stirring after 2, 4, 6 and 7 minutes. At end point all sugar should have dissolved, mixture should have bubbled vigorously all over surface, and formed a soft ball in cold water. Add vanilla (or other essence). Do not worry if mixture looks slightly curdled or buttery. Beat with a wooden spoon for about 5 minutes or until mixture loses its gloss and keeps its shape without flattening when poured onto a buttered metal surface. Let stand about an hour and then cut into squares. Mixture should be creamy, with melting texture. Fudge will be a little firmer the next day.
First Aid: If fudge will not set, reheat until whole mixture bubbles, stirring often. Cook 30 seconds longer, then beat again.

Candied Peel

This is a firm-textured confection, rather than a cooking ingredient.

4 mandarins
1 cup water
2 Tbsp water
¼ cup sugar
¼ cup castor sugar

Quarter mandarins. Peel away skins. (Use flesh for another purpose.) Cut each quarter lengthwise into two thinner strips. Put pieces in a heat resistant measuring cup with 1 cup of the water. Cover and boil for 15 minutes. Drain and pat dry. Put peel, sugar and remaining water into a high heat resistant casserole dish. Boil, uncovered, 3-4 minutes until sugar dissolves and forms a syrup which almost evaporates. Stop cooking before syrup turns golden. Lift hot pieces of peel out, one by one and turn them in castor sugar. Cool on a rack. Store in an airtight jar up to 2 weeks. Eat as a confection, plain or dipped in chocolate.

Caramel Peanuts

½ cup Roasted Peanuts (see page 19)
1 Tbsp water
¼ cup sugar

Prepare peanuts. In a small high-heat resistant microwave dish, heat the water and sugar on High (100% power) for about 3 minutes. Stir after 1 minute, then watch carefully, removing caramel as soon as it turns golden brown.
Add peanuts, heat for another minute, then stir until nuts are coated. On a buttered, metal surface form mixture into a bar or drop teaspoonfuls to make caramel peanut cluster. When cold, wrap in airtight wrap or store in an airtight jar.

Caramel Walnuts
Make Caramel Walnuts in the same way. Impale walnut halves on bamboo skewers and turn in hot caramel to coat. Twist skewer to lift it from each walnut.

Foolproof Fudge

Rich and smooth, nearly as good as well-made traditional fudge.

100g butter, cubed
¼ cup milk
2 tsp vanilla
4 cups sifted icing sugar
½ cup cocoa
about 1 cup walnut halves (optional)

Cut butter into 9 cubes. Arrange in a circle in a bowl or casserole dish. Add milk, vanilla, sifted icing sugar and cocoa on top. Microwave on High (100% power) for 2 minutes. Remove and beat mixture until smooth. Pour into a loaf pan or dish lined with sprayed greaseproof paper. Refrigerate overnight before cutting. Press a walnut half onto each piece of fudge when cutting it. Store in refrigerator.
Variation: Replace 1 tsp vanilla with 1 tsp rum essence.

Coconut Ice

This easy sweet will never set rock hard!

100g butter
¼ cup milk
1 tsp vanilla
4 cups sifted icing sugar
2 cups desiccated coconut
¾ tsp raspberry essence
4-6 drops red food colouring

Cut butter into 9 cubes. Arrange evenly around a flat-bottomed casserole, about 20-23cm. Add milk, vanilla and icing sugar. Cover and microwave on High (100% power) for 3 minutes, then beat until smooth. Stir in coconut and beat again. Spoon or pour half the mixture into a 16-18cm square pan lined with plastic or greaseproof paper. Smooth mixture. To the other half add raspberry essence and enough food colouring to make mixture pink. Beat to mix, then spoon over white mixture. Smooth with a knife or spatula. Refrigerate until firm. Cut in cubes and store in the refrigerator.

Dough Decorations

This dough can be shaped, baked, decorated and varnished in half an hour, if you work quickly.

1 cup flour
¼ cup salt
3-4 Tbsp hot water

Put flour and salt in a food processor fitted with metal cutting blade. Add 3 Tbsp hot tap water, then a little more if needed, to make a fairly firm dough (or mix dough in a bowl, adding water as necessary). Knead well, roll thinly, using a little flour on the board only if it sticks. Mould, twist or braid dough or cut into shapes with biscuit cutters or a pointed knife. If you are sticking on extra pieces, dampen before pressing in place. Make eyes, buttons, etc. with a skewer. Use skewer or plastic straw to make holes for attaching string and ribbons later.

Arrange on a plate or cardboard covered with a white paper towel. Put ½ cup water in microwave with dough decorations.

Bake cut out figures on Medium (50% power), allowing about 1 minute per piece, depending on size and thickness. Turn and rearrange pieces until they are hard, dry (and hot) on both sides. Paint with water or poster paints. Leave to dry for a few minutes, then arrange on newspaper and spray with clear polyurethane. Leave to dry, turn and spray again. Spray twice for an even, shiny coating, if desired OR paint with clear nail varnish.

Note: (a) Store dough in plastic bag in refrigerator for 1-2 weeks, if desired. (b) If it is not be painted, colour dough light brown using (dissolved) instant coffee.

Finger Paints

Small children apply these paints with great enthusiasm. Older children can create original gift wrapping paper!

2 Tbsp grated toilet soap
¼ cup warm water
2 Tbsp cornflour
1 Tbsp flour
1 cup cold water
food colourings

Grate the soap, using the end of partly used cakes, or the last slivers from several cakes. Mix with the warm water in a medium-sized bowl. Microwave on High (100% power) until soap dissolves and mixture bubbles up. In another bowl, mix cornflour, flour and cold water to form a smooth cream. Microwave 1-2 minutes, until mixture turns clear and thickens. Remove from heat and stir in soap mixture. Divide between four small dishes and add ¼-½ tsp of food colouring to each. Mix well. Cover. Use when warm or cold. Cover and refrigerate up to several days, warming before use, if too thick.

Note: (a) Concentrated food colouring on work surfaces and fingers may be removed by chlorine bleach. (b) Colours look much paler on paper than in containers.

Index